JAPAN FUND FOR PROSPEROUS AND RESILIENT ASIA AND THE PACIFIC USER GUIDE

JUNE 2022

ASIAN DEVELOPMENT BANK

ADB

Notes:
In this publication, "$" refers to United States dollars.

On the cover: For more than 20 years, the Japan Fund for Prosperous and Resilient Asia and the Pacific (JFPR) has been
providing direct grant assistance to the most vulnerable and marginalized people in underserved communities in
Asia and the Pacific. Photo shows children beneficiaries of JFPR G9107-LAO: Enhancing Capacity of Local Government
Agencies and Lao Women's Union for Sustainable Poverty Reduction in Northern Lao People's Democratic Republic
(photo by Jake Padua).

Contents

Tables

Abbreviations

ADB	–	Asian Development Bank
CC/DRM	–	climate change and disaster risk management
EOJ	–	Embassy of Japan
GOJ	–	Government of Japan
JFPR	–	Japan Fund for Prosperous and Resilient Asia and the Pacific
JICA	–	Japan International Cooperation Agency
Lao PDR	–	Lao People's Democratic Republic
PFM	–	public finance management
PR	–	poverty reduction
QII	–	quality infrastructure investment
SDCC	–	Sustainable Development and Climate Change Department
SDPF	–	Partner Funds Division
STG	–	sector and thematic group
TA	–	technical assistance
UHC	–	universal health coverage

Chapter I

INTRODUCTION

1. In September 2021, the Japan Fund for Poverty Reduction (JFPR) was renamed **Japan Fund for Prosperous and Resilient Asia and the Pacific** and enhanced to align the trust fund with Japan's current development priorities and consistent with the long-term corporate strategy of the Asian Development Bank (ADB). With the new priority areas that include universal health coverage, climate change and disaster risk management, quality infrastructure investment, and public finance management, in addition to poverty reduction, the fund will help ADB developing member countries to achieve resilient recovery from the ongoing pandemic crisis and enhance their preparedness for the next crisis. It will also help build sustainable societies and lay the foundations for a prosperous future while bolstering vulnerable groups. It is positioned as the next stage of work to help lift remaining populations above the poverty threshold and put others on a sustainable path to prosperity and resilience, building on the momentum of the fund's operation and achievements to further increase its development impact.[1]

2. As part of our efforts to make JFPR more "user friendly" and to continuously provide better service and support to JFPR's users and valuable clients, this **JFPR User Guide** is developed as a visual illustration on the requirements stipulated in the JFPR Implementation Guidelines. This user guide provides best practices, examples, tips, and suggestions to help JFPR users and clients tailor-fit their respective proposals in accordance with JFPR requirements to ensure smooth project processing and efficient project implementation.

---

[1] ADB. 2021. Japan Fund for Prosperous and Resilient Asia and the Pacific. Manila.

Chapter II

OBJECTIVE AND SCOPE

A. Priority Areas

Para. 4 of JFPR Implementation Guidelines

" The JFPR will put emphasis on prosperity and resilience. It will prioritize sovereign operation project grants and TA [technical assistance] that are focused on (i) universal health coverage; (ii) climate change and disaster risk management; (iii) quality infrastructure investment; (iv) public finance management, and (v) poverty reduction, unless otherwise agreed between GOJ [Government of Japan] and ADB. As these priority areas have cross-cutting features either in sectors or operational themes, it is encouraged that linkages across the priorities be established and highlighted in project proposals as appropriate. "

3.   In addition to the eligibility criteria set out in the "Specific Instructions on the Priority Areas" appended to the JFPR Implementation Guidelines, and to give better understanding on what is expected from each priority area, the following are sample JFPR projects for reference.

➲ Universal Health Coverage (UHC)

TA 9111-REG: Strengthening Developing Member Countries' Capacity in Elderly Care

◈   Why is the project eligible? – It conducted in-depth diagnostic studies on elderly care in recipient countries; assessed gaps in policies, programs, services, financing, and systems development in terms of aging; and identified future policy development and investment options.

TA 9701-MON: Improving Health Care Financing for Universal Health Coverage

◈   Why is the project eligible? – It assessed the current regulatory framework and purchasing practices in the health sector; developed an integrated purchasing system and a road map; and put in place a regulatory framework for the introduction and implementation of the strategic purchaser in Mongolia's health sector.

Grant 9200-VIE: Second Health Human Resources Development Project

◈ Why is the project eligible? – It implemented an innovative model that links health education and professional training institutions and local health-care facilities to improve direct health service delivery to poor and vulnerable groups and facilitate "bottom-up" reforms to health professional training programs. It also enhanced the quality of the health workforce in remote areas through a pilot project for the delivery of distance continuing medical education using mobile technologies and to equip health facilities to support the continuing medical education project.

⊃ Climate Change and Disaster Risk Management (CC/DRM)

TA 9993-THA: Climate Change Adaptation in Agriculture for Enhanced Recovery and Sustainability of Highlands

◈ Why is the project eligible? – It strengthened capacity to assess vulnerability to and the impacts of CC. It also determined factors contributing to CC vulnerability, analyzed baseline data and identified capacity needs and gaps in vulnerability in different agriculture subsectors, and trained local government staff on integrating CC concerns in agricultural and development plans.

Grant 9181-VAN: Cyclone Pam School Reconstruction Project

◈ Why is the project eligible? – It supported the rebuilding of junior secondary schools affected by the cyclone with "build back better" concepts to strengthen resilience to future disasters and CC risks and prepared schools and communities for climate and disaster risk management.

Grant 9187-MON: Strengthening Community Resilience to Dzud and Forest and Steppe Fires

◈ Why is the project eligible? – It strengthened community resilience to disaster risk by piloting an approach to develop community-based disaster risk management (DRM) plans, and supported implementation of selected disaster risk reduction measures by building small-scale disaster and climate-resilient structures, among others.

⮌ Quality Infrastructure Investment (QII)

TA 9503-CAM: Supporting Sustainable Integrated Urban Public Transport Development

◈   Why is the project eligible? – It improved management of an urban public transport system in Phnom Penh to achieve a sustainable integrated system and promote its use, such as through (a) developing policy guides and a planning toolkit for relevant public transport authorities, (b) formulating candidate integrated urban public transport improvement programs, and (c) providing capacity development training to the public transport authorities to improve their system management capacity.

⮌ Public Finance Management (PFM)

TA 9235-REG: Strengthening Tax Policy and Administration Capacity to Mobilize Domestic Resources

◈   Why is the project eligible? – It helped strengthen the capacity of tax authorities in the recipient countries to collect tax by (a) broadening and protecting the domestic tax base; (b) improving domestic tax compliance through efficient and transparent tax administration, enhanced exchange of information, and improved risk management practices; and (c) improving tools and procedures to stem both cross-border and domestic tax evasion and avoidance.

⮌ Poverty Reduction (PR)

Grant 9209-TIM: Coffee and Agroforestry Livelihood Improvement Project

◈   Why is the project eligible? – It improved the livelihoods of coffee farmers and piloted a new model for delivering extension services to smallholder coffee farmers. The project also strengthened industry management and supported initiatives to improve coffee quality and linkages with key markets.

Grant 9198-MON: Combating Domestic Violence Against Women and Children/ Grant 9221-MON: Combating Domestic Violence Against Women and Children – Additional Financing

◈   Why is the project eligible? – It strengthened the quality of and access to prevention and multidisciplinary response to domestic violence. It also supported women domestic violence survivors and persons with disabilities and reinforced the institutional capacity of stakeholders involved in the implementation of the revised Law on Combating Domestic Violence, through (a) increased access to and quality of response and protection such as model shelters; (b) capacity development for improved coordinated response, case management, and referral; (c) strengthening prevention, reporting, and survivor protection through the use of media and behavioral change communications; and (d) economic empowerment for survivors to inform the social welfare system in the future.

B. Use of Funds

⮑ Seed Money for Project Grants

Paras. 12–13 of JFPR Implementation Guidelines

" To facilitate the development of JFPR project grant proposals for poverty reduction support, SDPF [the Partner Funds Division] may approve financing up to $60,000 for its preparatory activities. The processing project officer may apply for Seed Money only after SDPF provides a clearance to proceed with proposal preparation and the concept paper has been approved. The Seed Money will be used to facilitate consultation with stakeholders, communities, and CSOs [civil society organizations] or promote collaboration that are necessary for a well-developed JFPR Grant Proposal. It may also to be used for conducting the required due diligence for the project. "

4.   All seed money applications should be submitted and processed through the JFPR Application and Project Monitoring System. To avoid connection problems, project teams should use **Internet Explorer** or **Google Chrome** when accessing the system. The quick reference guide in navigating the system can be found in this link. For more details, please also refer to the Seed Money Guidelines.

ADB JFPR Application and Project Monitoring System - Japan Fund for Prosperous and Resilient Asia and the Pacific

JFPR Application   Seed Money Application   Seed Money Monitoring

SUBMIT   PROCESS   REVIEW   APPROVE

Welcome to the Japan Fund for Prosperous and Resilient Asia and the Pacific Online Application System, an online tool for submitting fund application requests.

This site is open to all requestors who would like to submit JFPR fund applications. This site is for:

- Creation and Submission of Fund Application
- Seed Money Request (for JFPR poverty reduction stand-alone project grants only)
- Processing of Fund Application
- Review of Fund Application
- Approval of Fund Application

To guide you in navigating this system, refer to the quick reference guides (QRG) below:

- Fund Application
  - QRG for Project Officer
  - QRG for ED
- Seed Money
  - QRG for Seed Money Application
  - QRG for Seed Money Monitoring

5.   For consulting services, JFPR analysts[2] should be part of the project team and registered in ADB's Consultant Management System to avoid delays in the JFPR approval, and at the same time facilitate JFPR monitoring.

6.   Once the seed money application is approved, project teams should ensure that fund utilization is updated in the Seed Money Monitoring System. Contract variations should also be recorded and reflected in the Seed Money Monitoring System.

Year	Project Number	Project Name	DMC	Department	Approved Amount (in US$)	Approved Date	Expected Closing Date	Uncommitted Balance (in US$)	Undisbursed Balance (in US$)
2021	54360	Renewable Heating Demonstration in Remote Areas	MON	EARD	50,000.00	14 May 2021	14 Nov 2021	18,601.00	37,145.00
2020	53235	Farmer Group Market Access Development using Agriculture Technologies in Andhra Pradesh	IND	SARD	50,000.00	07 Feb 2020	07 Aug 2020	25,121.00	49,475.12
2020	53243	Community-Based Tourism COVID-19 Recovery Project	CAM	SERD	50,000.00	29 Jul 2020	29 Jan 2021	11,312.00	21,234.51
2019	52303	Managing Solid Waste in Secondary Cities	MON	EARD	50,000.00	31 May 2019	30 Nov 2019	80.00	1,686.54
2019	52374	Improving transport services in ger areas	MON	EARD	50,000.00	26 Apr 2019	26 Oct 2019	419.00	2,130.60

---

2 Refer to JFPR SharePoint for the JFPR focal persons.

Utilization

Staff Consultants

New Consultant

Contract No	Contract Name	Contract Amount (in US$)	Contract Commencement Date	Contract End Date	Disbursed Amount (in US$)	Disbursement Date	Contract Variation No	Contract Variation Date	Remarks	
		9,689.00	29 Aug 2020	31 Jan 2021			3	24 Feb 2021	Community Facilitator	☑ ➕ ✖
			29 Aug 2020	31 Jan 2021	4,665.49	16 Dec 2020	3	24 Feb 2021		➕ ✖
			29 Aug 2020	31 Jan 2021	4,780.00	31 Jan 2021	3	24 Feb 2021	Final claim - released on 10 Mar 2021	➕ ✖
		2,820.00	16 Sep 2020	31 Dec 2020			1	24 Feb 2021	Architecture/Engineer	☑ ➕ ✖
			16 Sep 2020	30 Oct 2020	2,820.00	23 Sep 2020				➕ ✖
		16,579.00	13 Nov 2020	15 Feb 2021			1	26 Jan 2021	Architecture/Engineer	☑ ➕ ✖
			13 Nov 2020	15 Feb 2021	2,475.00	17 Nov 2020	1	26 Jan 2021		➕ ✖
			13 Nov 2020	15 Feb 2021	5,775.00	06 Jan 2021	1	26 Jan 2021		➕ ✖
			13 Nov 2020	15 Feb 2021	8,250.00	15 Feb 2021	1	26 Jan 2021	The payment for final claim was released on 25 Feb 2021. However service was rendered within the contract completion date of 15 Feb 2021.	➕ ✖
		9,600.00	08 Mar 2021	30 Apr 2021					Professional legal service	☑ ➕ ✖

⤵ Administrative Budget Support for Project Grants

Para. 14 of JFPR Implementation Guidelines

❝ The implementing project officer is responsible for reporting the utilization of the administrative budget support and must provide SDPF at the end of each project year an update of its utilization. The implementing project officer is also responsible to ensure that utilization is within the approved amount. Any deviation from the proposed expenditures shall be consulted with and endorsed by SDPF. ❞

7.   All administrative budget support applications should be submitted and processed together with the project grant proposal documents. Below is the application template, which can be found in this link. Administrative Budget Support Guidelines provides more information.

JAPAN FUND FOR PROSPEROUS AND RESILIENT ASIA AND THE PACIFIC (JFPR)

ADMINISTRATIVE BUDGET SUPPORT APPLICATION
(For JFPR Project Grant Implementation Support)[1]

I.   **Rationale for Use of Administrative Budget Support**

1.   [Explain why the project needs additional budget resource beyond the regular administration budget provided by ADB. Cite project implementation complexities to support such request.]

2.   This additional budget support provided by JFPR for grant implementation is provided on an exceptional basis by the Government of Japan and is exclusive of the grant amount to be administered by ADB. The implementing project officer will manage and track the utilization of this budget and will provide the Partner Funds Division (SDPF) with an annual utilization update at the end of each project year. Any deviation from the proposed expenditures should be consulted with and endorsed by SDPF.

II.   **Administrative Budget Support Details**

Particulars	Details
Amount Requested	$
Justification	
Type of work to be rendered	

III.   **Cost Estimate of Administrative Budget Support**

Expenditure Category	Quantity	Unit	Rate / Unit	Total Costs

8.   For consulting services, JFPR analysts should be part of the project team and registered in ADB's Consultant Management System to prevent delays in obtaining JFPR approval as well as for JFPR monitoring purposes (footnote 2).

9.   Once the Administrative Budget Support is approved, project teams are responsible for the use of funds; details must be submitted annually to the SDPF via e-mail using the template below.

JFPR Administrative Budget Support - Utilization Report
as of 31 Dec 2021

1) PROJECT DETAILS	
Grant No.:	
Grant Name:	
Recipient DMC:	
Associated Loan/Project (if any):	
Grant Amt. ($):	
Admin. Budget Support Amt. ($):	
Grant Approval Date:	
Grant Commitment Date:	
Grant Effectivity Date:	
Grant Original Completion Date:	
Grant Revised Completion Date:	
Project Officer:	
Project Analyst:	
Department:	
Division:	

2) UTILIZATION

A. Consultants

Contract No.	Contract Name	Contract Amt.	Contract Commencement Date	Contract Completion Date	Disbursed Amt. ($)	Disbursement Date	Remarks

Total Contract Amt ($):   0
Total Disbursed Amt ($):   0

B. Other Expenditures

Type of Expenditures[a]	SDPF-JFPR Team Endorsement Date	Estimated Amt. ($)	Actual Expense Amt. ($)	Remarks

[a] Based from the GOJ-approved administrative budget support.

Total Estimated Amt ($):   0
Total Actual Expense Amt ($):   0

TOTAL COMMITTED BALANCE: 0
TOTAL DISBURSEMENTS: 0

Chapter III

APPLICATION AND APPROVAL PROCESS

A. Donor Coordination and Japanese Visibility

Paras. 21–22 of JFPR Implementation Guidelines

"To ensure harmonization and smooth coordination with donor's policies and programs, project officer will consult with the Embassy of Japan (EOJ) and Japan International Cooperation Agency (JICA). The summary of consultation with EOJ and JICA shall be included in the proposal submitted to SDPF."

"The project officer is highly encouraged to utilize Japan's human resources, expertise, financial resources, and technologies through the collaboration with JICA, Japanese CSOs, private sector, and academic institutions."

10.   To supplement the Guidance Note on Coordination with EOJ and JICA, the project team must consult with the local EOJ and JICA office of the recipient country prior to the official submission of the JFPR application, as this is one of the criteria for concept clearance, and to avoid further delay in the project's processing timeline.

11.   In addition to the Guidance Note on Japanese Visibility, the following are tips on how to identify possibilities for Japanese visibility in the proposal. Table 1 shows examples of the Japanese visibility measures presented in the proposals adopted in past and ongoing JFPR projects.

  (i)   Refer to Japan's Official Development Assistance (ODA) Rolling Plan[3] and JICA's ODA Portfolio[4] for the recipient country to identify possibility for cofinancing and synergies with JICA and other bilateral assistance.

  (ii)   Discuss the proposal with the local EOJ and JICA office to identify possibilities for collaborations as well as Japanese agencies/institutions and experts who could be tapped to participate in the project.

---

3 Ministry of Foreign Affairs of Japan. https://www.mofa.go.jp/policy/oda/index.html.
4 Japan International Cooperation Agency. https://www.jica.go.jp/english/countries/index.html.

(iii)   Identify how Japanese technology, knowledge, and experience can be utilized in the project.

Table 1: Examples of Japanese Visibility Measures Extracted from Final Project Proposals

⊃ **Collaborative Activities with JICA** (i.e., yen loans, grants, and TA)

Project Name	Description
TA 9554-REG: Southeast Asian Services Facility **(For CAM: Support for Improved Sanitation through the Development of City-wide Inclusive Sanitation for Phnom Penh)**	Collaboration between JICA and ADB will provide a holistic approach to the development of city-wide inclusive sanitation in Phnom Penh. The **ongoing JICA Project for Capacity Development for Sewage Management in Phnom Penh Capital Administration and Ministry of Public Works and Transport** commenced in April 2019 and **mainly supports the development of sewered sanitation. ADB's JFPR-funded TA, on the other hand, has a stronger focus on support for legal, financial, and technical capacity development and the development of city-wide inclusive sanitation using non-sewered sanitation solutions** to complement the proposed sewerage development.
TA 8590-PHI: Enhancing Capacities for the KALAHI-CIDSS National Community-Driven Development Project	JICA will be closely consulted in the design and implementation of the TA. The proposed TA will **draw lessons from the capacity development needs of the recently completed JICA-funded Autonomous Region in Muslim Mindanao Social Fund for Peace and Development.** In addition, the proposed TA will make **use of the community-based DRM training manual produced as an output of the JICA technical cooperation project on Disaster Risk Reduction and Management Capacity Enhancement.**
TA 9300-CAM: Institutional Capacity Building in the Road Sector	JICA has already provided two weigh stations to control axle load. Now, it is installing two more mobile weigh scales at both ends of the Tsubasa Bridge, which was completed in 2015, and is preparing an instruction manual to maintain and monitor the operation of such weigh stations. Further, JICA is planning to provide eight more state-of-the-art weigh stations on National Highway 5 in the near future. The **TA will utilize the proposed JICA training programs in the Project for Strengthening Capacity and Maintenance for Roads and Bridges** conducted by the government as part of the executing agency's action plan under the TA's output 1.
TA 6537-BHU: Improving Market Linkages for Cottage and Small Industries	The **national certification level to be established under the TA will be helpful in marketing the products promoted under JICA's Community Entrepreneurial and Capacity Development Project.** In addition, the **entrepreneurs trained in Japan under JICA's project will be included in the TA's capacity-building programs/activities.** The TA will further **explore potential areas for collaboration with JICA specifically to learn from Japan's "one village one product" experience.**

continued on next page

Table 1 *continued*

Project Name	Description
• Grant 9208-MON: Support for Inclusive Education	Possible opportunities for **collaboration have been identified with JICA, especially in further dissemination of materials prepared under the recently completed Strengthening Teachers' Ability and Reasonable Treatments for Children with Disabilities (START) Project (2015–2019).** The project team collaborated with the JICA project design mission for START II at the end of 2019 to ensure synergies. Continuous coordination will take place through Mongolia's Inclusive Education Coordination Mechanism, comprising representatives of EOJ in Mongolia and JICA, who were consulted during the project design process.

⮎ Utilization of Japanese Human Resources (e.g., JICA experts/volunteers, Japanese NGOs, GOJ officials, and academic/research institutions)

Project Name	Description
• TA 8435-REG: Trade Facilitation in South Asia	The participation of **officials from GOJ (Customs and Tariff Bureau), and representatives from the academe and business sectors in Japan, who will serve as resource persons/international experts, in workshops and meetings of the South Asia Subregional Economic Cooperation Customs Subgroup,** will be explored and pursued. The TA will also promote partnership between and among ADB, GOJ (Customs and Tariff Bureau of the Ministry of Finance), and the World Customs Organization.
• TA 6539-REG: Investing in Climate Change Adaptation through Agroecological Landscape Restoration: A Nature-Based Solution for Climate Resilience	The TA will seek to **engage Japanese experts, research institutes, think tanks, and nongovernment organizations (NGOs)** to incorporate **good practices of sustainable and climate-resilient agriculture practices and increased value addition of ecological agri-food products in Japan, as well as use of high-level technologies, such as remote sensing and other satellite technologies, in capacity development and case studies.** Potential contributors are the **United Nations University Institute for the Advanced Study of Sustainability, with respect to the International Partnership for the Satoyama Initiative, the National Institute for Environmental Studies, the Graduate School of Regional Resource Management of University of Hyogo, and the Japan Aerospace Exploration Agency (JAXA).**
• TA 6636-IND: Enhancing Community Participation, Gender Mainstreaming, and Institutional Capacity Building of Uttar Pradesh Power Corporation Limited	Possibilities for **JICA volunteers to collaborate in JFPR TA-funded initiatives were discussed and will be pursued during TA implementation.** After the TA is approved, a formal request will be made through JICA's New Delhi office to assign a volunteer to work with TA consultants in developing community-based approaches to improve bill collections.

continued on next page

Table 1 *continued*

Project Name	Description
	The **proposed applied learning and exposure program to Japan** for senior and middle management professionals from the Uttar Pradesh Power Corporation Limited **will enhance awareness of Japanese technical standards and business practices in electricity distribution among staff. This will promote future collaboration between Japanese utilities and Japanese technology providers and electricity supply industry** in Uttar Pradesh India.
• Grant 9208-MON: Support for Inclusive Education	There is **potential for Japan Overseas Cooperation Volunteers to support implementation of local level activities** and work closely with the four area coordinators in the project's three aimags (provinces) and one district of Ulaanbaatar. The project team will coordinate with the focal point in Ulaanbaatar to see whether an opportunity can materialize. **Volunteers have been placed in Mongolia's rural schools in the past.** Details can be finalized during the grant inception phase.
• Grant 9204-MON: Improving Transport Services in Ger Areas	**Japanese resource persons will be encouraged to participate in the project,** particularly consultants who were **involved with JICA's project, Promoting Social Participation of Persons with Disabilities in Ulaanbaatar,** and can provide insight into the findings and their applicability to this grant and improving accessibility in public transport.

⮌ Utilization of Japanese Technology, Knowledge, and Experience
(e.g., Japanese private companies and organizations)

Project Name	Description
• TA 8800-PAK: Balochistan Water Resources Development	The project has an innovative concept of **developing a water resources information system (WRIS) for Balochistan through an advanced Japanese technology that has been piloted by JAXA.** Applying it, **TA experts will provide government officials with a customized training program that will use an innovative satellite-based data system** for (i) rainfall (10 km grid, up to hourly); (ii) soil moisture (up to daily); (iii) surface temperature; (iv) meteorological drought index (10 km grid, up to daily); (v) a vegetation index; and (vi) land cover maps. It will conduct geospatial analyses for water resource management based on available data identifying climatic zones. This **Japanese technology can be used for the government's other pipeline projects,** which will be financed by donors including JICA. During the TA implementation, a **relevant workshop, at which JAXA and other concerned Japanese experts on satellite remote sensing, GIS, and WRIS will serve as resource persons,** will be held to disseminate the technology in Pakistan.

continued on next page

Table 1 *continued*

Project Name	Description
• TA 6669-REG: Promoting Action on Plastic Pollution from Source to Sea in Asia and the Pacific – Prioritizing and Implementing Actions to Reduce Marine Plastic Pollution (Subproject 2)	Japan is a world leader in this field and has mature systems and technologies for integrated solid waste management (ISWM) that incorporate 3R (reduce, reuse, recycle) and circular economy approaches. As such, it is important to the **outcomes of the TA that the target developing member countries benefit from Japanese experience and technologies,** combined with those available approaches and technologies from the participating countries and others. This **Japanese knowledge and experience would be utilized initially to design pilot projects appropriate for the communities, to inform the design of the different components (solid waste collection, transport, recycling),** and **in the equipment to be used – e.g., designing a compact ISWM system, low-energy small garbage collection trucks appropriate for small communities, plastic recycling, and Japanese technology for plastics to fuels/oils.** **Japanese experts on ISWM and circular economy technologies will be invited to participate in the TA's numerous regional forums to share this knowledge and showcase Japanese technologies,** including at the Healthy Oceans Technology and Innovation Forum (Q4 2020, ADB HQ). **Japanese technologies could also feature in a key TA knowledge product on infrastructure, technology, and investment needs for Asia and the Pacific for transitioning to a circular economy. The Japanese private sector will also be invited to participate through the TA consulting/contracting opportunities,** and, further, the **TA promotes and supports investments (sovereign and nonsovereign) in ISWM and the circular economy, which will provide more opportunities to apply Japanese technologies in the region.**
• Grant 9172-BAN: Pilot Project on Weather Index-Based Crop Insurance	The TA will assess available infrastructure and enhance capacity to ensure a smooth flow of standardized, reliable data from accredited weather stations. This involves upgrading weather stations and preparing maintenance plans to improve the near-real-time weather data collection and reporting system. Related training will be offered to the Bangladesh Meteorological Department, the Bangladesh Water Development Board, and other concerned agencies. In addition, **to improve the accuracy of weather data, the use of space technology through remote sensing will be explored in collaboration with JAXA.**

continued on next page

Table 1 *continued*

Project Name	Description
• Grant 9210-IND: Addressing Urban Transport Needs of Vulnerable Women and Differently Abled	**Visibility of Japanese aid and technology will also be ensured through** (i) attendance of a representative from EOJ and JICA at every major event of the grant supported by the trust fund, with press coverage, such as during the distribution of assistive aids, the felicitation of female e-rickshaw drivers and taxi drivers, and the inauguration of public toilet blocks; (ii) systematic use of trust fund logos on grant-related correspondence, workshop material and banners, and any media publication; (iii) clear reference to the financial contribution of GOJ during major project activities and for major outputs (publications, press releases, and speeches); and (iv) **exploration of the use of Japanese technologies such as fully automated, self-composting toilets and projects implemented by JICA in India.** For example, Tafgard Technology for Environment Friendly Toilets will offer good practice case studies for the design and construction of public toilets around Regional Rapid Transit System stations.

ADB = Asian Development Bank, DRM = disaster risk management, EOJ = Embassy of Japan, GOJ = Government of Japan, JICA = Japan International Cooperation Agency, km = kilometer, TA = technical assistance.
Source: Authors.

B.   Application Process

> ### Para. 23 of JFPR Implementation Guidelines
>
> " Proposals will be processed upon receipt through the JFPR Application and Project Monitoring System. The process described in this section are specific to the application and funding approval from the Government of Japan. The project teams are expected to comply with the standard ADB due diligence and parallel process for ADB approval. "

12.   All JFPR proposals should be submitted and processed through the JFPR Application and Project Monitoring System. Project teams should use **Internet Explorer** or **Google Chrome** when accessing the system to avoid connection problems. The quick reference guide in navigating the system can be found in this link.

C. Coordination Mechanisms with SDCC's Sector/ Thematic Groups

Para. 24 of JFPR Implementation Guidelines

❝To facilitate a harmonized approach and facilitate a streamlined review process, project teams shall consult with the relevant sector/thematic groups (STGs) and include them as peer reviewer to ensure eligibility of their proposal following the criteria stipulated in the Specific Instructions on the Priority Areas prior to the online submission of the proposal concept.❞

13.   The following are things to remember in coordinating with STGs:

    (i)   E-mail confirmation from the STG's focal to SDPF that the proposal is eligible under JFPR's priorities should be included in the submission of the initial concept.

    (ii)   The STG focal person for the specific priority area should be included as a peer reviewer to ensure that the proposal has been reviewed and that their inputs are incorporated and that it meets the eligibility criteria.

Table 2: Priority Area Focal Persons

Priority Area[a]	Focal Persons of STGs in SDCC[b]
Universal Health Coverage	Patrick Osewe, Arindam Dutta
Climate Change and Disaster Risk Management	Charlotte Benson (Adaptation), Arghya Sinha Roy (Mitigation)
Quality Infrastructure Investment	Hyun Chang Park
Public Finance Management	Jose Luis Syquia, Rachana Shrestha

[a] For "poverty reduction," no coordination mechanism with STGs is required. The initial concept should be provided directly to the SDPF-JFPR Team.
[b] As of June 2022.

D. Required Documents for Project Grants

Paras. 25–28 of JFPR Implementation Guidelines

❝The processing project officer shall submit to SDPF an approved or draft project concept paper using the applicable ADB template together with a supplementary document and confirmation of eligibility by the relevant STGs.❞

❝The processing project officer submits a draft Grant Assistance Report or the Attached JFPR Project Grant proposal to SDPF and a meeting among SDPF, the Advisor of the Executive Director for Japan and the processing project officer will be arranged to discuss the project design, as necessary. The processing project officer submits the final grant proposal package to Director, SDPF with a memo signed by the relevant Director General.❞

14.   Table 3 lists the documents required for a project grant. Moreover, JFPR project grant templates can be found in the Board Document System, and a template for the "initial JFPR proposal checklist" can be found on the JFPR SharePoint Page.

Table 3: List of Project Grant Required Documents

Project Grant Type	Concept Stage	Proposal Stage
Stand-alone	Draft concept paper and supplementary document (i)	Approved concept paper Draft GAR and linked documents
Attached to an ADB investment project	Approved concept paper of the ADB project and supplementary document (i)	Draft RRP, PAM, and attached JFPR linked document

GAR = grant assistance report, JFPR = Japan Fund for Prosperous and Resilient Asia and the Pacific, PAM = project administration manual, RRP = report and recommendation of the President.
Note: (i) Initial JFPR Proposal Checklist.
Source: ADB. 2022. Japan Fund for Prosperous and Resilient Asia and the Pacific Implementation Guidelines. Manila.

15.   Here are some tips when preparing the JFPR project grant proposal.

(i)   Ensure that the storyline is clear, cohesive, and reader-friendly. For attached JFPR project grants, clear explanation should be provided as to how the project grant will support and complement ADB's investment loan. Moreover, outputs/activities under the JFPR project grant should be identified in the overall loan's design and monitoring framework (DMF).

(ii)   Look into lessons and best practices from previous JFPR projects and how these can be adopted in the proposal.

(iii)   Coordination with EOJ and JICA in the recipient country is a must since this will be one of the fundamental considerations when the proposal is submitted to GOJ for approval.

(iv)   Ensure that Japanese visibility measures are adopted in the project.

(v)   Identify outputs to be funded by JFPR in case of multiple fund sources to ensure delineation of activities and no overlapping of support.

(vi)   As much as possible, fact-finding must be conducted before the proposal stage.

(vii)   Ensure realistic approval dates based on the JFPR project grant's processing workflow.

(viii)   Observe JFPR citation rules. If JFPR funding has not been approved by GOJ, indicate in a footnote **"JFPR is a possible funding source subject to the approval by the Government of Japan"** the first time JFPR is mentioned in the document.

16.   For the supplementary documents, please take note of the following:

(i)   In the initial JFPR proposal checklist, information should be for <u>JFPR's support only</u>, especially when the project will be supported by different funding sources. Moreover, the checklist should clearly present details on (a) coordination with EOJ and JICA (i.e., names of staff consulted, date of consultation, outcome of discussion, such as confirmation of support on the proposal and suggestions, etc.); and (b) concrete measures on Japanese visibility to be adopted in the project.

(ii)   For JFPR project grants attached to ensuing loans, an expanded DMF specifically for JFPR's support should be provided. This is for JFPR's internal review process and for GOJ's information only and can be excluded in the ADB approval process.

(iii)   The detailed cost estimates table is extracted from the project administration manual (PAM).

17.   For the final submission memo, sample templates are provided below for reference. The list of attachments can be updated as needed.

➲ *Stand-Alone Project Grant*

ADB
Asian Development Bank

Memorandum
{Department}
{Division}

Date

To: Director, SDPF

Through: {Director General, User Department}

From: {Director, User Division}

Subject: **Project No.: Project Grant Name**
               —Request for Japan Fund for Prosperous and Resilient Asia and the Pacific Financing

---

1.   We request you to submit the proposed {project grant name} to the Government of Japan for the approval of financing from the Japan Fund for Prosperous and Resilient Asia and the Pacific in the amount of $XX million.

2.   The attached Grant Assistance Report and supporting documents have incorporated comments provided by SDCC's Partner Funds Division and have been cleared by the Japanese Executive Director's Office.

Attachments: a/s

cc: Director General concurrently Chief Compliance Officer, SDCC; JFPR Team, SDPF; {other CC list}

⊃ *Attached to an ADB Investment Project*

ADB

Asian Development Bank

Memorandum
{Department}
{Division}

Date

To: Director, SDPF

Through: {Director General, User Department}

From: {Director, User Division}

Subject: **Project No.: Project Grant Name**
            —Request for Japan Fund for Prosperous and Resilient Asia and the Pacific Financing

1.   We submit for approval of the Government of Japan under the Japan Fund for Prosperous and Resilient Asia and the Pacific (JFPR) financing the proposed {project grant name} in the amount of $XX million. The proposed JFPR project grant is attached to the proposed {ADB project name} which will be funded by a loan from the Asian Development Bank (ADB). The JFPR project grant will be administered together with the ADB loan.

2.   The attached (i) draft JFPR grant proposal and supporting documents, (ii) draft RRP, and the draft PAM have been revised to incorporate comments from the Japanese Executive Director's Office and SDCC's Partner Funds Division.

Attachments: a/s

cc: Director General concurrently Chief Compliance Officer, SDCC; JFPR Team, SDPF; {other CC list}

E. Required Documents for Technical Assistance

Paras. 29–31 of JFPR Implementation Guidelines

"The processing project officer shall submit to SDPF the applicable ADB TA template together with a supplementary document."

"The processing project officer submits a draft TA proposal using the applicable ADB TA template together with two supplementary documents to SDPF and a meeting among SDPF, the Advisor of the Executive Director for Japan, and the processing project officer will be arranged to discuss the TA proposal, as necessary. The processing project officer submits the final TA proposal package to Director, SDPF with a memo signed by the relevant Director General."

18.   Table 4 lists the documents required for TA. Templates for the applicable ADB reports can be found in the Board Document System. Templates for the supplementary documents can be found on the JFPR SharePoint Page.

Table 4: List of Technical Assistance Required Documents

TA Type	Concept Stage	Proposal Stage[a]
KSTA	Draft KSTA concept paper and supplementary document (i)	Approved concept paper,[b] draft KSTA report, and supplementary documents (ii) and (iii)
TRTA (*for project preparation*)	Draft TRTA report and supplementary document (i)	Drafts project concept paper, TRTA report, and supplementary documents (ii) and (iii)
TRTA (*for capacity development/policy advice*)	Draft TRTA report and supplementary document (i)	Drafts RRP, TRTA report, and supplementary documents (ii) and (iii)
KSTA Cluster[c]	Draft KSTA subproject report and supplementary document (i)	Approved concept paper, drafts KSTA Cluster report, KSTA subproject report, and supplementary documents (ii) and (iii)
TRTA Cluster[c]	Draft TRTA subproject report and supplementary document (i)	Drafts TRTA Cluster report, project concept paper, TRTA subproject report, and supplementary documents (ii) and (iii)
TRTA Facility[c]	Draft TRTA report and supplementary document (i)	Drafts TRTA facility report, project concept paper, TRTA report, and supplementary documents (i) and (ii)
Increase in TA amount		Draft memo or draft Board document[d] and supporting documents (ii), (iii), and (iv)

GOJ = Government of Japan, KSTA = knowledge and support technical assistance, RRP = report and recommendation of the President, TA = technical assistance, TRTA = transaction technical assistance.
[a]   JFPR's review is required prior to interdepartmental review.
[b]   To be included only in the final proposal package for submission to GOJ.
[c]   JFPR's support is earmarked to a specific project.
[d]   If Board approval is required per Staff Instruction on Business Processes for TRTA and KSTA.
(i)   Initial JFPR Proposal Checklist
(ii)   Detailed JFPR Proposal Checklist
(iii) Detailed Cost Estimates Table
(iv) Project Description Document
Source: ADB. 2022. Japan Fund for Prosperous and Resilient Asia and the Pacific Implementation Guidelines. Manila.

19.   Here are some tips for when preparing the JFPR TA proposal.

(i)   Ensure that the storyline is clear, cohesive, and reader-friendly. For attached JFPR TAs, clear explanation should be provided as to how the TA will support and complement ADB's investment project. Moreover, outputs/activities under the JFPR TA should be identified in the overall loan's DMF.

(ii)   Look into lessons and best practices from previous JFPR projects and how these can be adopted in the proposal.

(iii)   Coordination with EOJ and JICA in the recipient country is a must since this will be one of the fundamental considerations when the proposal is submitted to GOJ for approval.

(iv)   Ensure that Japanese visibility measures are adopted in the project.

(v)   Identify outputs to be funded by JFPR in case of multiple fund sources to ensure delineation of activities and no overlapping of support.

(vi)   As much as possible, fact-finding must have been conducted before the proposal stage.

(vii)   Ensure realistic approval dates based on the JFPR TA's processing workflow.

(viii)   Observe JFPR's citation rules. If JFPR funding has not been approved by GOJ, please indicate in a footnote ***"JFPR is a possible funding source subject to the approval by the Government of Japan"*** the first time JFPR is mentioned in the document.

20.   For the supplementary documents, please take note of the following:

(i)   In the initial and detailed JFPR proposal checklists, information should be for JFPR's support only especially when the project will be supported by different funding sources. Moreover, the checklist should clearly present details on (a) coordination with the local EOJ and JICA office (i.e., names of staff consulted, date of consultation, outcome of discussion, etc.); and (b) concrete measures on Japanese visibility to be adopted in the project.

(ii)   Estimated cost allocation per output should be provided in the initial JFPR proposal checklist.

(iii)   In the detailed cost estimates table, please ensure that the total is accurate. Project teams should be reminded that, for JFPR TA, non-consultant costs should be minimal. In addition, please be reminded of the following:

» If goods/equipment will be requested, please make sure that the cost breakdown in the "Goods" table is consistent with the main cost estimates table. This also applies to the cost breakdown in the "Workshops/Trainings/Seminars" table.

» In the "Workshops/Trainings/Seminars" table, please refrain from indicating "TBD". If venue, number of participants, and/or duration are not yet final, indicative information will suffice.

» If "miscellaneous administration and support costs" and "others" are requested, please add a footnote on the possible expenditures under these budget items.

21.   For the final submission memo, below is a sample template for reference. The list of attachments can be updated as needed.

ADB

Asian Development Bank

Memorandum
{Department}
{Division}

Date

To:	Director, SDPF
Through:	{Director General, User Department}
From:	{Director, User Division}
Subject:	**Project No.: TA Name** **—Request for Japan Fund for Prosperous and Resilient Asia and the Pacific Financing**

1.   We request you to submit the proposed {TA type} for {TA name} to the Government of Japan for approval of financing from the Japan Fund for Prosperous and Resilient Asia and the Pacific in the amount of $XX million.

2.   The attached technical assistance report and supporting documents incorporate the comments provided by SDCC's Partner Funds Division and have been cleared by the Japanese Executive Director's Office.

Attachments: a/s

cc: Director General concurrently Chief Compliance Officer, SDCC; JFPR Team, SDPF; {other CC list}

Chapter IV

PROJECT IMPLEMENTATION ARRANGEMENTS

A. Requirements Upon Approval

Paras. 36–37 of JFPR Implementation Guidelines

"A signing and/or launching ceremony, with the attendance of EOJ and JICA is highly encouraged. The implementing project officer shall inform EOJ and JICA - through the resident mission - at least 10 working days before the scheduled date. News release shall be drafted in consultation with the Department of Communications and the resident mission will invite local and international press for the ceremony."

"The project implementation officer must schedule a briefing with SDPF to discuss donor requirements from the project prior to the Inception Mission/Workshop so the project team can relay to the executing and implementing agencies. The implementing project officer must ensure Japanese visibility and local awareness of JFPR in the recipient country/ies throughout the project's implementation period."

22. Below is a sample photo of a signing/launching ceremony with attendance from EOJ and JICA, and a sample news release on the approval of a JFPR-funded project.

23.   Upon effectiveness of the JFPR-funded project, the project officer is expected to have a briefing with SDPF to discuss the donor requirements, specifically on the coordination with EOJ and JICA and Japanese visibility during project implementation, to be relayed to the project's consulting team and executing and implementing agencies during the inception mission/workshop.

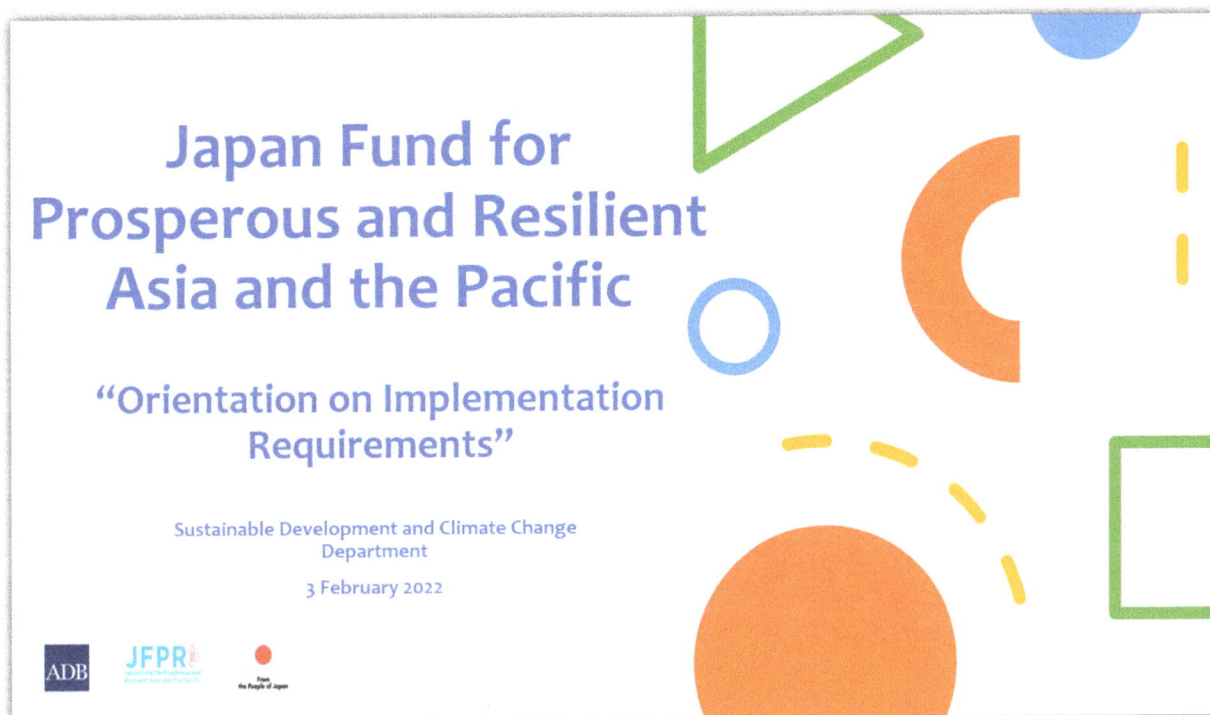

B. Policies Governing Project Implementation

Paras. 39–42 of JFPR Implementation Guidelines

" The JFPR-financed project's implementation, supervision, and monitoring will be conducted by the user departments following ADB's applicable policies, procedures, and guidelines, including consulting services and procurement, disbursement, social and environmental safeguards, financial management and reporting, and anticorruption and governance. During implementation, SDPF will assist the user departments in monitoring, advice, and capturing lessons learned. "

24.   Generally, project teams will implement JFPR projects in accordance with relevant ADB policies unless specific provisions are included in the JFPR Implementation Guidelines, such as:

- Any change in implementation will require prior consultation and e-mail concurrence from SDPF.

- Exemption to ADB's universal procurement policy.

- International travel as an ineligible expenditure.

- ADB implementation of JFPR project grant components is not allowed.

C. Monitoring

Para. 43 of JFPR Implementation Guidelines

"The implementing project officer will carry out ADB's fiduciary responsibilities for project implementation, in accordance with ADB standards. Implementing project officer will be responsible for monitoring the performance in accordance with PAI [Project Administration Instruction] 5.08 on Project Performance Monitoring. BTORs [back-to-office reports] shall be uploaded as well in eOperations. SDPF will refer to this system for the status of the JFPR projects."

25.   Below is a screenshot on how BTORs of JFPR-funded projects should be uploaded in eOperations.

D. Reports

Para. 44 of JFPR Implementation Guidelines

" Submission of completion reports for JFPR will be in accordance with ADB's PAI 6.07 for project grants and PAI 6.08 for TA. A *record of Japanese visibility measures* including all knowledge products produced under the JFPR projects *shall be listed and reported in their completion reports.* The draft completion report shall be shared with SDPF for comments. The approved completion report must be disclosed in the ADB website and submitted to SDPF for forwarding to GOJ. "

26. Project teams should ensure that the Japanese visibility measures presented in the proposal approved by GOJ are adhered to during implementation, and these should be recorded in the completion reports. If needed, these should include an appendix highlighting the Japanese visibility adopted, such as photos showing the JFPR logo in workshops, on publications, on equipment purchased, etc., or engagement of Japanese experts as resource persons in knowledge sharing events, among others. The following are examples of completion reports that have included Japanese visibility measures adopted throughout the project.

(i) TA 8435-REG: Trade Facilitation in South Asia

ADB

Completion Report

Project Number: 47016-001
Technical Assistance Number: 8435
May 2020

Trade Facilitation in South Asia

This document is being disclosed to the public in accordance with ADB's Access to Information Policy.

Asian Development Bank

(SCS) and its Trade Facilitation and Transport Working Group (TFTWG), and SASEC Secretariat; and (iii) nodal officials and focal points in each of the member countries. The TA engaged a total of 65.5 person-months of international consultants and 183.1 person-months of national consultants. Upon approval, 33.5 person-months of international consultants and 34 person-months of national consultants were planned. However, this was significantly increased during the implementation of the TA to cover the additional activities. The consultants were recruited as individual consultants following the *Guidelines on the Use of Consultants* by ADB. The consultants delivered satisfactory performance, with some rated as excellent.

All activities supported by JFPR were consistently highlighted as funding source. The JFPR logo was shown in all event banners and posted in all documentation. Attribution was always made during opening and closing remarks of ADB at all relevant events, which were showcased on the SASEC website, with JFPR noted as funding source. Other visibility measures implemented by the TA include among others, (i) participation as resource person of Mr. Norikazu Kuramoto of Japan's Ministry of Finance, during the Third SASEC Meeting in Goa, India in March 2015; and (ii) participation by JICA and JETRO officials during the SASEC TFTWG held in Tokyo, Japan in November 2015.

(ii)   Grant 9181-VAN: Cyclone Pam School Reconstruction Project

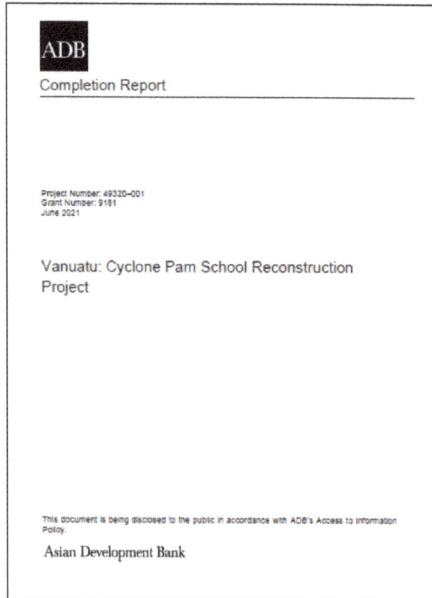

ADB

Completion Report

Project Number: 49320-001
Grant Number: 9181
June 2021

Vanuatu: Cyclone Pam School Reconstruction
Project

This document is being disclosed to the public in accordance with ADB's Access to Information Policy.

Asian Development Bank

ASIAN DEVELOPMENT BANK
6 ADB Avenue, Mandaluyong City
1550 Metro Manila, Philippines
Tel +63 2 632 4444
Fax +63 2 636 2444
www.adb.org

NEWS RELEASE

21 February 2020

**ADB, Japan, and Vanuatu Commission
Climate Resilient Schools in Tanna**

TANNA, VANUATU (21 February 2020) — The Asian Development Bank (ADB) joined the Governments of Vanuatu in a commissioning ceremony today to open several junior secondary schools that were built back better following damage by Cyclone Pam in 2015.

Vanuatu's Minister of Education and Training Jean-Pierre Niroa led the official opening ceremonies for the schools. Senior Country Coordination Officer from ADB's Vanuatu Pacific Country Office, Nancy Wells, Japan's Ambassador to Vanuatu Harumi Katsumata, and the project team joined local communities in officially opening the Imaki, Ianasia, and Kwataparen schools.

The Cyclone Pam School Reconstruction Project built 57 new buildings and refurbished 33 existing ones—a total of 90 buildings, which were built back better with climate resilient features. These structures are already helping 4 communities in Tanna, providing quality education to residents, especially children.

"The schools that were rebuilt under the project will be safer and will provide a cleaner learning environment for students," said Ms. Wells. "The schools have climate resilient features, including dormitories which can be converted into community shelters during a disaster."

The four schools targeted by the project were rebuilt and upgraded with facilities such as emergency power back-up and communications systems, as well as tanks for storing rainwater.

Capacity building was a key component of the project through which local laborers had the opportunity to build their skills in concreting, carpentry, and painting.

The Japan Fund for Poverty Reduction, a financing facility provided by the Government of Japan, provided a $8 million grant for the project.

ADB is committed to achieving a prosperous, inclusive, resilient, and sustainable Asia and the Pacific, while sustaining its efforts to eradicate extreme poverty. Established in 1966, it is owned by 68 members—49 from the region.

---

10.   The new facilities were designed to harvest rainwater, enabling increased water storage capacity essential to provision and improved performance of water, sanitation and hygiene (WASH) facilities. Solar lighting, backup power, paved walkways, and security and privacy fencing contributed to improved functionality. The dormitories and associated WASH and other facilities (showers, laundry, toilets, and ablution blocks) helped boost the boarding capacity of schools from 237 male and 227 female students to 320 male and 320 female students, a 39% increase. The official opening ceremony for the four schools, held on 21 February 2020, was attended by Vanuatu's caretaker Minister of Education, Japan's Ambassador to Vanuatu, and ADB staff. Near project closing, the project team utilized the remaining available funds to procure furniture, further improving the utility and functionality of the schools (Appendix 3).

Japanese Visibility Photos

Project billboard, Imaki Junior Secondary School (Photo by Contractor: China Civil Engineering Construction Corporation).

Unveiling of plaque at Imaki Junior Secondary School. (*From left to right*) ADB Senior Country Coordination Officer Nancy Wells, Ambassador of Japan Her Excellency Harumi Katsumata, Minister of Education and Training of the Government of Vanuatu Jean-Pierre Niroa (Photo by Contractor: China Civil Engineering Construction Corporation).

27.   Project teams should ensure that EOJ and the JICA office are updated on the project's status as this will help in mitigating possible risks specifically in terms of donor relations. Further, project teams may also invite EOJ and JICA officials to knowledge sharing events and activities under the JFPR-funded project.

E. Dissemination of Results

Para. 47 of JFPR Implementation Guidelines

" The implementing project officer is encouraged to disseminate as widely as possible, in-country and within ADB, the project outcomes and lessons from implementation. If feasible, case studies, beneficiary stories, video documentation, or other forms of media be produced, and seminars be conducted. The implementing project officer is also required to provide SDPF a copy (e.g., printed or electronic) of all knowledge products to be delivered under JFPR TAs and ensure that Japanese visibility is reflected. "

28.   The following are examples on how to disseminate the results from JFPR-funded projects. Detailed examples of knowledge products produced from past and ongoing JFPR projects are in Appendix 1.

➲ Project Videos

Grant 9166-SAM: Community Sanitation Project

Better Sanitation Improves Lives in Samoa

Video | 15 September 2017

SHARE THIS PAGE

Water-borne diseases like diarrhea are a serious problem in Samoa.

0:00 / 3:06

Better Sanitation Improves Lives in Samoa

Improved sanitation is having a significant impact on the quality of life of Samoans.

Better Sanitation Means Better Health in Samoa.

Grant 9184-MYA: Economic Empowerment of the Poor and Women in the East–West Economic Corridor[5]

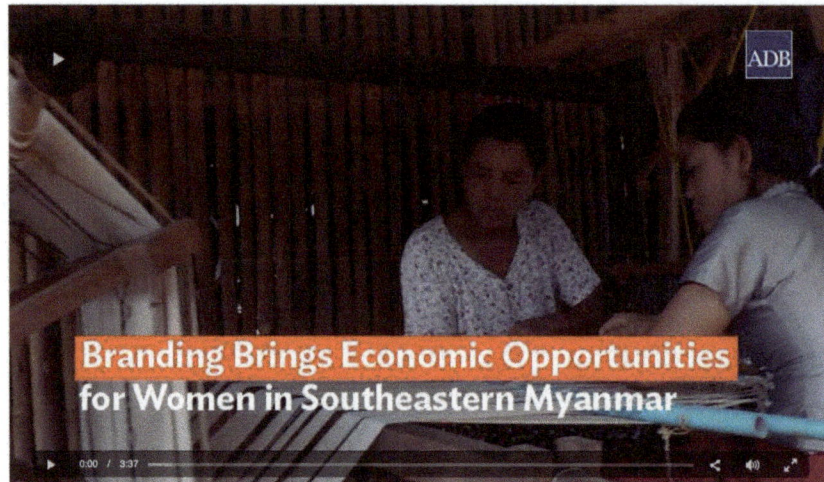

Branding Brings Economic Opportunities for Women in Southeastern Myanmar

Video | 27 August 2019

SHARE THIS PAGE

WATCH: Branding Brings Economic Opportunities for Women in Southeastern Myanmar

In Myanmar, ADB through a grant from the Japan Fund for Poverty Reduction initiated branding project for local handicraft.

ADB is partnering with Japan Fund for Poverty Reduction in Myanmar.

---

[5] ADB has temporarily placed on hold all sovereign project disbursements and new contracts since 1 February 2021.

➲ Case Studies

PROJECT RESULT / CASE STUDY

Five years after the Nepal earthquake – building back better schools for a safer future

ADB

April 2020

ADB's Earthquake Emergency Assistance Project in Nepal, jointly financed by ADB, US Agency for International Development (USAID), and the Government of Nepal, financed the rebuilding of quality schools to withstand future disasters.

Pratima Khadka (third from left) and her friends enjoy learning in a new classroom. (Photo by Narendra Shrestha)

DHULIKHEL , NEPAL – Fourteen-year-old Pratima Khadka is all smiles when she describes her new has modern facilities," she says. "The teachers regularly use multimedia projectors in the classro more fun and interesting."

Khadka and her family, like millions of others, were affected by the devastating earthquake that magnitude quake, one of the biggest in Nepal's history, resulted in the tragic loss of life of aroun schools and 30,000 classrooms were damaged or destroyed, directly affecting the education of 1

"Limiting the lost education time for these students, and returning them to quality schools built were the goals of the school reconstruction project supported by the Asian Development Bank (A project officer at ADB's Nepal Resident Mission.

Keeping students in school

With her school badly damaged, Khadka continued learning at temporary learning classrooms (T and tarpaulin shelter was cramped and had only basic conditions. "While the TLCs did provide o we could see children were dropping out, especially girls coming from far off areas," says Loken Sanjiwani Secondary School where Pratima studies. "We knew we had to build the permanent st the students as well get back to the pre-earthquake enrollment numbers."

After more than 4 years since the fatal earthquake, Prime Minister of Nepal Mr. K.P. Sharma Oli reconstructed Sanjiwani Secondary School in Dhulikhel to the community at a ceremony on 24 A

Grant 9180-NEP: Disaster Risk Reduction and Livelihood Restoration for Earthquake-Affected Communities

PROJECT RESULT / CASE STUDY

Mongolia Battles to Save its Peatlands, and a Nomadic Way of Life

ADB

May 2018

A tenuous ecological balance is fracturing as Mongolia's peatlands succumb to climate change, over-grazing, and industrial activity.

Livestock numbers in Mongolia have risen sharply since the 1990s, straining the ecological balance at peatlands like this one in central Mongolia. (Credit: Nyambayar Batbayar)

Arkhangai Province, Mongolia -- For millennia the wetlands of the Orkhon Valley have nourished the livestock and livelihoods of herders like Chimedregzen Nadmid, who has lived there all his life.

He remembers when the land was so boggy that riding a horse was impossible. The soil absorbed water like a sponge, forming a vast plain of peatlands that sprouted thick grass and fed lakes and rivers. It was harsh terrain but ideal pastureland.

Then a couple of decades ago it changed. Marshy wetlands shrank and grass vanished. The corrugated landscape flattened and dried out. "The first thing I noticed was the falling water level," says Chimed, as he is known. "I knew I had to do something."

A fractured ecological balance

Peatlands form when dead plant matter partially decomposes in marshy areas, capturing carbon taken from the air by the plants when alive. The moist, rich soil is a magnet for herders as much of the country's land is exhausted from over-grazing or desertification. As a result, peatlands are suffering the same fate. They're also being damaged by mining, road construction, and human-caused steppe fires. Climate change is making matters worse.

A tenuous ecological balance is fracturing. Peatlands are Mongolia's last fertile pastures. Undisturbed, they absorb water from melting snow and rain which they filter and release into rivers and lakes. They prevent soil erosion and maintain groundwater levels that sustain crops and forests while staving off desertification.

"The first thing I noticed was the falling water level. I knew I had to do something."

Chimedregzen Nadmid

But the area covered by peat in Mongolia has almost halved in the past 50 years. This has had a dramatic impact on permafrost—huge lenses of frozen ground left by ancient glaciations. When peat degrades,

TA 8802-MON: Strategic Planning for Peatlands

⟳ Blogs

TA 9201-MON: Gender-Responsive Sector and Local Development Policies and Actions

Asian Development Blog
Straight Talk from Development Experts

TOPICS   COUNTRIES/ECONOMIES   AUTHORS

GENDER

Who Milks the Cow Now? Or How to Communicate Gender Stereotypes

A man milking a cow breaks a gender stereotype in Mongolia. Photo by

By Pinky Serafica, Tsolmon Begzsuren

Changing gender stereotypes in tectonic plates of gender equalit

Монгол хэл дээр унших бол энд дарь

The picture looks benign enough: A ma the reins of two calves. Unless you are #normal, peering from the multi-colore herding cattle, goats and sheep. Woma housework. So wait, man milking cow?

Asian Development Blog
Straight Talk from Development Experts

TOPICS   COUNTRIES/ECONOMIES   AUTHORS

AGRICULTURE AND FOOD SECURITY   FINANCE SECTOR DEVELOPMENT

Crop Insurance Lessons from My Field Trip to Rajshahi

Rajshahi farmers need modern technology to lift productivity and incomes. Photo by Sadharan Bima Corp.

Subscribe to Newsletter

By Arup Kumar Chatterjee

Crop insurance is a valuable climate adaptation tool for disaster-prone countries like Bangladesh.

My destination was Rajshahi, located on the north bank of the Padma River in Bangladesh, near the border with India. Here one can understand what more likely than not roused Rabindranath Tagore to compose the song *Amar Shonar Bangla* (My Golden Bengal).

Maybe Tagore, like me, encountered the fully-bloomed paddy fields, the aroma of the mango forests, and the splendid fire of a hundred dusks unchallenged by a solitary cloud.

Unfortunately, Bangladesh is also highly exposed to extreme weather events and prone to flash flooding, drought, cyclones, and saltwater inundation due to tidal surges. With the very sustainability of agriculture at risk, it can adversely impact livelihoods and cause food insecurity.

Grant 9172-BAN: Pilot Project on Weather Index-Based Crop Insurance

⊃ Photo Essays

Bridge Transforms Lives of Isolated Villagers in Tajikistan

Photo Essay | 29 May 2013

SHARE THIS PAGE

In 2007, through the Japan Fund for Poverty Reduction (JFPR), improve access, mobility and communication for over 47,000 vi

In Tajikistan, a new bridge built by ADB under a J connecting once isolated villagers to urban amer has already saved lives in medical emergencies, businesses.

Grant 9111-TAJ: Sustainable Access for Isolated Rural Communities

Young Survivors Graduate from School after Typhoon Yolanda

Photo Essay | 1 June 2015

SHARE THIS PAGE

Bislig Elementary School in the Philippines' province of Leyte begins another school year today. Badly damaged by Typhoon Yolanda in 2013, the school is well on its way to full recovery, having graduated its first class after the disaster in March 2015. The story of young survivor Honeylette Molina, who finished at the top of the class, demonstrates that natural catastrophes can take lives, destroy buildings and livelihoods, but these cannot break the human spirit and the desire to succeed.

Grant 9175-PHI: Emergency Assistance and Early Recovery for Poor Municipalities Affected by Typhoon Yolanda

⟳ Publications

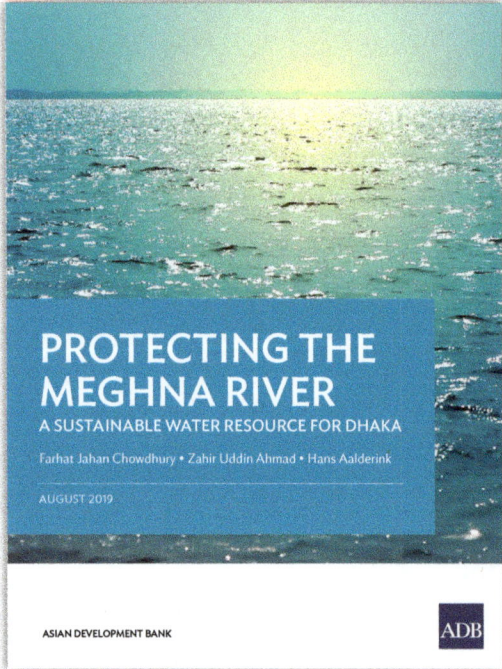

PROTECTING THE MEGHNA RIVER
A SUSTAINABLE WATER RESOURCE FOR DHAKA

Farhat Jahan Chowdhury • Zahir Uddin Ahmad • Hans Aalderink

AUGUST 2019

ASIAN DEVELOPMENT BANK

Protecting the Meghna River
A Sustainable Water Resource for Dhaka

This publication explores the potential of the Meghna River as an alternative water source for Dhaka. It also describes the fragile state of the city's current drinking water supply due to increasing demand and surface contamination. The authors assess the threats facing the Meghna River and identify protection measures needed to ensure that it can provide a sustainable and safe supply of drinking water. These measures include designating ecological critical areas, promoting cleaner industrial production, monitoring pollution, controlling wastewater discharges and pesticide use, and empowering local stewardship of the river.

About the Asian Development Bank

ADB is committed to achieving a prosperous, inclusive, resilient, and sustainable Asia and the Pacific, while sustaining its efforts to eradicate extreme poverty. Established in 1966, it is owned by 68 members —49 from the region. Its main instruments for helping its developing member countries are policy dialogue, loans, equity investments, guarantees, grants, and technical assistance.

ASIAN DEVELOPMENT BANK
6 ADB Avenue, Mandaluyong City
1550 Metro Manila, Philippines
www.adb.org

TA 8803-BAN: Strengthening Monitoring and Enforcement in the Meghna River for Dhaka's Sustainable Water Supply

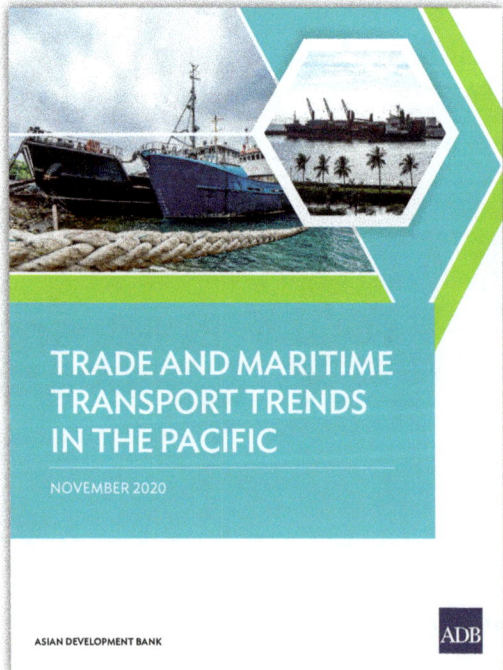

TRADE AND MARITIME TRANSPORT TRENDS IN THE PACIFIC

NOVEMBER 2020

ASIAN DEVELOPMENT BANK

Trade and Maritime Transport Trends in the Pacific

This study seeks to help fill knowledge gaps on maritime trade in the Pacific. It examines trade flows in Fiji, Papua New Guinea, Samoa, Timor-Leste, Tonga, and Vanuatu. The study looks at shared constraints, such as the effects of climate change and exposure to external shocks, and identifies synergistic and regional approaches to address them. It aims to inform long-term planning for trade facilitation across the region by identifying key questions for governments and development partners to consider. It also addresses core questions including how trade flows in the region are changing, how growth will impact seaport operations and shipping services, and how trade efficiency can be improved.

About the Asian Development Bank

ADB is committed to achieving a prosperous, inclusive, resilient, and sustainable Asia and the Pacific, while sustaining its efforts to eradicate extreme poverty. Established in 1966, it is owned by 68 members —49 from the region. Its main instruments for helping its developing member countries are policy dialogue, loans, equity investments, guarantees, grants, and technical assistance.

ASIAN DEVELOPMENT BANK
6 ADB Avenue, Mandaluyong City
1550 Metro Manila, Philippines
www.adb.org

TA 8674-REG: Trade and Transport Facilitation in the Pacific

⇌ Infographics

Grant 9183-MON: Integrated Livelihood Improvement and Sustainable Tourism Khuvsgul Lake National Park

Grant 9174-MYA: Enhancing Rural Livelihoods and Incomes

➲ Stories

Securing Sustainable Income while Protecting the Environment

A grant from the Japan Fund for Poverty Reduction has empowered marginalized fisherfolks in Indonesia and the Philippines to run their own alternative businesses while protecting the Coral Reef Triangle.

Eco-Friendly Earnings. Ecosystem-based and financially viable businesses have increased the incomes of fisherfolks in two coastal communities in Palawan, Philippines and East Kalimantan, Indonesia.

PROJECT
Regional: Developing Sustainable Alternative Livelihoods in Coastal Fishing Communities in the Coral Triangle: Indonesia and Philippines

PROJECT COST
$2 million

- Financing Partner
  - Japan Fund for Poverty Reduction **$2 million**

APPROVAL DATE
November 2011

SIGNING DATE
15 May 2012

COMPLETION
October 2019

Grant 9160-REG: Developing Sustainable Alternative Livelihoods in Coastal Fishing Communities in the Coral Triangle

Improving River Basin Management

Threatened by climate change, the Pyanj River Basin is now the center of climate-proofing activities, thanks to a collaborative project by ADB and the Japan Fund for Poverty Reduction.

Resilient River Basin. Lives and livelihoods of people dependent on the Pyanj River Basin in Tajikistan have a more secure future as the basin becomes better protected and climate-proofed.

PROJECT
Water Resources Management in the Pyanj River Basin Project

PROJECT COST
$33.7 million

- ADB **$25 million**
- Tajikistan **$3.7 million**
- Financing Partner
  - Japan Fund for Poverty Reduction **$5 million**

APPROVAL DATE
September 2016

SIGNING DATE
15 Nov 2016

COMPLETION
June 2024

Grant 9188-TAJ and TA 9183-TAJ: Water Resources Management in the Pyanj River Basin Project

Chapter V

SUMMARY

29.   As a summary, the following are takeaways and useful tips in processing and implementing JFPR project/s.

Stage	Things to Keep in Mind
A. General	(i) Get to know the SDPF–JFPR Team

International Staff

HIROKI KASAHARA
hkasahara@adb.org

YUSUKE SEKIGUCHI
ysekiguchi@adb.org

SHO TABATA
stabata@adb.org

National Staff

RHINA TOLENTINO
rlopez@adb.org

Administrative Staff

REBECCA CANOY
rcanoy@adb.org.

ELLA ARIENDA
earienda@adb.org

(ii)   Familiarize yourself with the JFPR SharePoint Page, including
- JFPR Application and Monitoring System
- JFPR Implementation Guidelines
- Specific Instructions on the Priority Areas
- Processing Workflows
- List of Document Requirements for Submission and Templates
- Guidance Note on Japanese Visibility
- Guidance Note on Coordination with EOJ and JICA
- JFPR logo

Stage	Things to Keep in Mind
B. Processing	(i) Ensure coordination with the relevant STGs to ensure eligibility under JFPR's priority areas and ensure that the project does not duplicate other efforts in the recipient country.
	(ii) Be mindful of the target approval, and plan the project processing schedule accordingly.
	(iii) Consult with EOJ and JICA to confirm there is no overlapping and duplication of activities, and explore possible synergies with EOJ and JICA's projects.
	(iv) Consult with other multilateral development banks as well as other bilateral donors to ensure complementation of efforts.
	(v) Ensure the commitment of the recipient government, executing and implementing agencies, and other stakeholders to the objectives and approach proposed under the project before proposal submission.
	(vi) Make sure there will be no substantial changes (i.e., scope, outputs and activities, and cost allocation) to the proposal endorsed by GOJ. Major changes may require GOJ's reassessment and reapproval and could delay ADB approval.
C. Implementation	(i) Implementation will be in accordance with ADB policies and guidelines unless specific provisions are stipulated in the JFPR Implementation Guidelines.
	(ii) Prior consultation and concurrence are necessary from SDPF before any changes are introduced.
	(iii) Ensure that the Japanese visibility measures presented in the endorsed proposal are adhered to.
	(iv) As much as possible, produce knowledge products for dissemination and visibility.
	(v) Inform SDPF of forthcoming missions for which Executive Director for Japan's Office, GOJ, and JFPR Team participation may be desirable (i.e., key project events such as facility inaugurations, turnover of equipment, completion workshops/missions, etc.). The JFPR Team may also be invited to key review missions in which its advice or inputs are required.
	(vi) When in doubt, consult with the JFPR Team.

ADB = Asian Development Bank, EOJ = Embassy of Japan, GOJ = Government of Japan, JFPR = Japan Fund for Prosperous and Resilient Asia and the Pacific, JICA = Japan International Cooperation Agency, SDPF = SDCC's Partner Funds Division, STG = sector/thematic group.
Source: ADB. 2022. Japan Fund for Prosperous and Resilient Asia and the Pacific Implementation Guidelines. Manila.

30.   Project teams are encouraged to like and follow the Facebook and Instagram accounts of **ADB Japan Funds**, to follow actions in the field.

adbjapanfunds

Examples of Knowledge Products Produced from JFPR Projects (2004–2021)

A. Project Videos

Project Name	Approval Year	Sector	Project Description and Japanese Visibility/ Collaboration
Project Grants			
G9201-PHI: Emergency Assistance for Reconstruction and Recovery of Marawi	2018		The emergency assistance will provide the Government of the Philippines with immediate and flexible financing to implement programs, projects, and activities included in the Bangon Marawi Comprehensive Rehabilitation and Recovery Program.
			ADB. 2020. Hope Amid the Rebuilding – ADB's Marawi Support. Video. https://www.adb.org/news/videos/hope-amid-rebuilding-adb-s-marawi-support.
Grant 9196-IND: Enabling and Skilling Communities for Sustainable Water Services in West Bengal	2018		The project will provide safe and sustainable drinking water as per the standards set by the Government of India to over 1.65 million people in the arsenic-fluoride- and salinity-affected selected areas of Bankura, North 24 Parganas, and Purba Medinipur districts of West Bengal (project districts). It will introduce an innovative and sustainable institutional framework and advanced technology for smart water management to enable efficient service delivery in project districts.
			ADB. 2020. Innovative Drinking Water Project Sets New Standards in Rural West Bengal. Video. https://www.adb.org/news/videos/innovative-drinking-water-project-sets-new-standards-rural-west-bengal.
			Pokhrel, N. 2019. For Rural Water Systems, Small and Simple is a "Pipe Dream". Asian Development Blog. Manila: ADB. https://blogs.adb.org/blog/rural-water-systems-small-and-simple-pipe-dream.
G9185-MYA: Emergency Support for Chin State Livelihoods Restoration[a]	2016		The project helped restore the livelihoods of communities in Chin State, where numerous landslides disrupted the fragile transport links between mountainous villages and severely damaged community assets after Cyclone Komen in 2015.
			ADB. 2020. ADB Builds Resilience for Chin State Livelihoods in Myanmar. Video. https://www.adb.org/news/videos/adb-builds-resilience-chin-state-livelihoods-myanmar.

Project Name	Approval Year	Sector	Project Description and Japanese Visibility/ Collaboration
G9184-MYA: Economic Empowerment of the Poor and Women in East–West Economic Corridor[a]	2015		The project sought small businesses along an East–West Economic Corridor by providing skills training, technology, and finance to help the poor and women set up sustainable crafts and food product businesses targeted at tourists. ADB. 2019. Branding Brings Economic Opportunities for Women in Southeastern Myanmar. Video. https://www.adb.org/news/videos/branding-brings-economic-opportunities-women-southeastern-myanmar.
G9183-MON: Integrated Livelihoods Improvement and Sustainable Tourism in Khuvsgul Lake National Park	2015		The project will support local livelihoods through improved capacity for sustainable tourism and subsistence activities, improved waste management services, and the establishment of grazing zones for herder groups. ADB. 2020. ADB Promotes Community-Based Ecotourism in Mongolia. Video. https://www.adb.org/news/videos/adb-promotes-community-based-ecotourism-mongolia.
G9180-NEP: Disaster Risk Reduction Restoration for Earthquake-Affected Communities	2015		The project will improve equity and enhance social inclusion in the earthquake-affected districts and the disaster preparedness and resilience of earthquake-affected communities by (i) constructing/rebuilding model disaster-resilient schools; (ii) providing a microcredit facility for livelihood restoration to small farmer cooperatives; and (iii) strengthening DRM capacity of the affected communities. ADB. 2020. Building a Better Future – Five Years after the Nepal Earthquake. Video. https://www.adb.org/news/videos/building-better-future-five-years-after-nepal-earthquake.
G9176-MYA: Greater Mekong Subregion Capacity Building for HIV/AIDS Prevention	2013		The project contributed toward achieving the Millennium Development Goal targets by reversing/managing the spread of HIV/AIDS in Myanmar by increasing the coverage and quality of information and services (prevention, treatment, and care) for targeted populations along and near the economic corridors. ADB. 2020. Strengthening HIV/AIDS Prevention in Myanmar. Video. https://www.adb.org/news/videos/strengthening-hivaids-prevention-myanmar.
G9175-PHI: Emergency Assistance and Early Recovery for Poor Municipalities Affected by Typhoon Yolanda	2013		The project will mitigate the adverse social and economic impacts on the poor resulting from Typhoon Yolanda in the Eastern Visayas through (i) restoring local government unit infrastructure and providing access to emergency employment and livelihood support; (ii) providing basic emergency maternal and child health care services; and (iii) improving resilience to future disasters and effective project management, coordination, monitoring, and reporting. ADB. 2014. Typhoon Yolanda One Year On: Relief, Recovery and Reconstruction. Video. https://www.adb.org/news/videos/typhoon-yolanda-one-year-relief-recovery-and-reconstruction.

Project Name	Approval Year	Sector	Project Description and Japanese Visibility/ Collaboration
G9174-MYA: Enhancing Rural Livelihoods and Incomes[a]	2013		The project provided one consolidated investment grant of $12 million to target four diverse geographic (and agro-ecological) regions in Myanmar to implement different interventions based on topography, agricultural production systems, and natural resource management regimes focusing on two interrelated sets of activities: (i) improvements and upgrades of social and productive infrastructure; and (ii) improvement of capacities of communities and project line agencies at the local and state levels, and to a lesser degree at the central levels. ADB. 2019. Enhancing Rural Livelihoods in Myanmar. Video. https://www.adb.org/news/videos/enhancing-rural-livelihoods-myanmar.
G9166-SAM: Community Sanitation Project	2012		The project will provide vulnerable households sustainable access to better sanitation in targeted regions of Samoa by establishing and piloting an innovative delivery method and institutional arrangements for providing subsidized sanitation infrastructure to low-income households. ADB. 2017. Better Sanitation Improves Lives in Samoa. Video. https://www.adb.org/news/videos/better-sanitation-improves-lives-samoa.
G9162-PHI: Promoting Partnership and Innovations in Poor and Underserved Communities	2012		The project will pilot a viable model for strengthening strategic multisectoral partnerships to support the sustainable development of poor and underserved communities that can be replicated in the Philippines and other developing member countries of ADB through (i) piloting a program for expanding multisectoral partnerships; (ii) improving access to basic services, including economic and livelihood opportunities; (iii) enhancing capacities of residents in community development and social entrepreneurship; and (iv) establishing an effective project management, monitoring and evaluation, and reporting system. Community-Managed Potable Water System in Southville 7, Laguna. YouTube Video. https://www.youtube.com/watch?v=8-88TjQuDfM. ADB. 2016. Making Resettlement Work through Partnerships. Case Study. Manila: ADB. https://development.asia/case-study/making-resettlement-work-through-partnerships.
G9158-REG: Improving Women's Access to Clean and Renewable Energy in Bhutan, Nepal, and Sri Lanka	2011		The project will increase access for poor rural women and other vulnerable groups to affordable and reliable clean and renewable energy sources and technologies by providing small hydropower systems, teaching them about clean and renewable energy technology, and training women as electricians and technicians. ADB. 2016. Power Line Maintenance Means Jobs for Women in Bhutan. Video. https://www.adb.org/news/videos/power-line-maintenance-means-jobs-women-bhutan.

Project Name	Approval Year	Sector	Project Description and Japanese Visibility/Collaboration
G9155-BHU: Advancing Economic Opportunities of Women and Girls	2011		The project will establish effective partnerships between government, NGOs, and the private sector for the economic empowerment of women through capacity building and sustaining economic activities and employment for women. ADB. 2015. It's a Woman's Business in Rural Bhutan. Video. https://www.adb.org/news/videos/its-womans-business-rural-bhutan.
G9149-BHU: Upgrading Schools and Integrated Disaster Education (UPSIDE) in Bhutan	2010		The project will develop a model safe learning environment and enhance people's DRM capacity in Mongar and Trashigang, the two most affected districts, through (i) restoration and improvement of four heavily damaged primary schools; (ii) strengthened DRM capacity through school-based DRM and community-based DRM training and planning; and (iii) project management, monitoring, and evaluation. ADB. 2017. Rebuilding Schools in Eastern Bhutan. Video. https://www.adb.org/news/videos/rebuilding-schools-eastern-bhutan.
G9139-MON: Demonstration Project for Improved Electricity Services to the Low-Income Communities in Rural Areas	2009		The project will improve the quality of life of the residents of bag centers (the smallest administration unit) in Mongolia by providing reliable electricity supply to remote communities. ADB. 2013. ADB Helps Mongolians Keep Warm. Video. https://www.adb.org/news/videos/adb-helps-mongolians-keep-warm.
G9135-NEP: Establishing Women and Children Service Centers	2009		The project will reduce vulnerability and helplessness of women and children in five rural districts of Nepal by providing professional and coordinated protection and assistance to female and child victims of crimes such as rape, domestic violence, polygamy, allegations of witchcraft, child abuse, child marriage, and trafficking. ADB. 2019. Police and Community Partner in Nepal's Effort to Tackle Violence Against Women. Video. https://www.adb.org/news/videos/police-and-community-partner-nepal-s-effort-tackle-violence-against-women.
G9115-MON: Access to Health Services for Disadvantaged Groups in Ulaanbaatar	2007		The project will improve access to health services for vulnerable groups in Ulaanbaatar, through their full participation in the design and management of support programs for the provision of health services. ADB. 2013. In Mongolia, a Chance for Those Who Need It Most. Video. https://www.adb.org/news/videos/mongolia-chance-those-who-need-it-most.

Project Name	Approval Year	Sector	Project Description and Japanese Visibility/ Collaboration
G9043-TAJ: Community Participation and Public Information Campaign for Health Improvement	2004		The project will improve access to and use of innovative health-care procedures promoted under the Health Sector Reform Project by the poor population, particularly the poorest women of reproductive age, mothers, and children, by strengthening public information on and community and family participation in determining, implementing, and monitoring health needs, practices, and services. ADB. 2012. Living with the Pyanj River: Flood Mitigation in Tajikistan. Video. https://www.adb.org/news/videos/living-pyanj-river-flood-mitigation-tajikistan.
Technical Assistance			
TA6854-REG: Improving Water Security and Resilience through Digitalization – Improving Water Security and Resilience through Digitalization (Subproject 2)	2021		The TA will support the achievement of the TA cluster outcome of resilient investments and policies in the water sector by raising the awareness and improving the capacity of selected municipal and village governing bodies, utilities, or water resource management entities, or other water-related organizations and agencies on resilience. ADB. 2021. aRe yoU Water Resilient?. Video. https://www.adb.org/news/videos/are-you-water-resilient.
TA6782-IND: Enhancing Market Linkages for Farmer Producer Organizations	2021		The TA, attached to the Maharashtra Agribusiness Network Project, will support farmer producer organizations by improving a network of post-harvest marketing and value chains focusing on specific horticulture crops. ADB. 2021. Improving Productivity and Lives of Farmers in India's Maharashtra State. Video. https://www.adb.org/news/videos/improving-productivity-and-lives-farmers-india-s-maharashtra-state.
TA9323-LAO: Sustainable Rural Infrastructure and Watershed Management Sector Project	2017		The project will address issues of project readiness improvement and watershed management in mountainous provinces of Northern Lao PDR by using an integrated land use planning approach that integrates efficient, sustainable, and climate-resilient rural infrastructure, and feasible watershed protection measures. ADB. 2020. Project Readiness Improvement Trust Fund: Promoting Readiness of Climate Resilient Investments in Southeast Asia. Video. https://www.adb.org/news/videos/project-readiness-improvement-trust-fund-promoting-readiness-climate-resilient-investments.

Project Name	Approval Year	Sector	Project Description and Japanese Visibility/ Collaboration
TA9204-THA: Strengthening Integrated Water Resource Planning and Management at River Basin Level	2016		The TA will improve overall efficiency of the water management system in 25 river basins by (i) establishing the base river basin integrated water resource management modeling tool; and (ii) strengthening capacity of river basin personnel in river basin integrated planning. ADB. 2015. From Upstream to Downstream, Thailand Responds to Climate Change. Video. https://www.adb.org/news/videos/upstreamdownstream-thailand-responds-climate-change.
TA8623-BHU: Adapting to Climate Change through Integrated Water Resources Management	2014		This capacity development technical assistance project will support the National Environment Commission and other relevant government agencies to implement specific elements of the 2011 Water Act and related Water Regulation (to be approved) and promote IWRM to facilitate effective river basin management and strengthen resilience to current variability and anticipated impacts of future climate change. Development Asia. 2019. Taking a Sustainable and Holistic Approach to Water Resources Management. Manila: ADB. https://development.asia/case-study/taking-sustainable-and-holistic-approach-water-resources-management. *(Case study includes a video entitled "Climate Adaptive Water Resources")*

Legend: = Agriculture, Natural Resources, and Rural Development   = Multisector

      = Education   = Public Sector Management

      = Energy   = Water and Other Urban Infrastructure and Services

      = Health

DRM = disaster risk management, NGO = nongovernment organization, TA = technical assistance.

[a] ADB has temporarily placed on hold all sovereign project disbursements and new contracts since 1 February 2021.

Source: Authors.

B. Infographics

Project Name	Approval Year	Sector	Project Description and Japanese Visibility/ Collaboration
Project Grants			
G9185-MYA: Emergency Support for Chin State Livelihoods Restoration Project[a]	2016		The project helped restore the livelihoods of communities in Chin State, where numerous landslides disrupted the fragile transport links between mountainous villages and severely damaged community assets after Cyclone Komen in 015. ADB. 2020. Emergency Support for Chin State Livelihoods Restoration Project in Myanmar. Infographic. https://www.adb.org/news/infographics/emergency-support-chin-state-livelihoods-restoration-project-myanmar.
G9184-MYA: Economic Empowerment of the Poor and Women in the East–West Economic Corridor[a]	2015		The project sought small businesses along an East–West Economic Corridor by providing skills training, technology, and finance to help the poor and women set up sustainable crafts and food product businesses targeted at tourists. ADB. 2019. Economic Empowerment of the Poor and Women in the East-West Economic Corridor in Myanmar. Infographic. https://www.adb.org/news/infographics/empowerment-poor-women-east-west-economic-corridor-myanmar.
G9183-MON: Integrated Livelihoods Improvement and Sustainable Tourism in Khuvsgul Lake National Park	2015		The project will support local livelihoods through improved capacity for sustainable tourism and subsistence activities, improved waste management services, and the establishment of grazing zones for herder groups. ADB. 2020. Integrated Livelihoods Improvement and Sustainable Tourism in Khuvskul Lake National Park. Infographic. https://www.adb.org/news/infographics/integrated-livelihoods-improvement-and-sustainable-tourism-khuvskul-lake-national.
G9174-MYA: Enhancing Rural Livelihoods and Incomesa	2013		The project provided one consolidated investment grant of $12 million to target four diverse geographic (and agro-ecological) regions in Myanmar to implement different interventions based on topography, agricultural production systems, and natural resource management regimes focusing on two interrelated sets of activities: (i) improvements and upgrades of social and productive infrastructure; and (ii) improvement of capacities of communities and project line agencies at the local and state levels, and to a lesser degree at the central levels. ADB. 2019. Enhancing Rural Livelihoods and Incomes in Myanmar. Infographic. https://www.adb.org/news/infographics/enhancing-rural-livelihoods-and-incomes-myanmar.

Project Name	Approval Year	Sector	Project Description and Japanese Visibility/ Collaboration
G9175-PHI: Emergency Assistance and Early Recovery for Poor Municipalities Affected by Typhoon Yolanda	2013		The project will mitigate the adverse social and economic impacts on the poor resulting from Typhoon Yolanda in the Eastern Visayas through (i) restoring local government unit infrastructure and providing access to emergency employment and livelihood support; (ii) providing basic emergency maternal and child health care services; (iii) and improving resilience to future disasters and effective project management, coordination, monitoring, and reporting. ADB. 2014. Typhoon Yolanda (Haiyan): ADB's Response. Infographic. https://www.adb.org/news/infographics/typhoon-yolanda-haiyan-adbs-response.
Technical Assistance			
TA9230-MON: Sustainable Tourism Development Project	2016		The TA will support the Government of Mongolia for in preparing a proposed loan, the Sustainable Tourism Development Project, which aims to transform two national parks in Khuvsgul and Khentii aimags (provinces) as models for economically inclusive tourism and conservation in the protected area network, by improving park infrastructure, sanitation, and capacity to sustainably manage tourism growth. ADB. 2022. Sustainable Tourism Development Project in Mongolia. Infographic. https://www.adb.org/news/infographics/sustainable-tourism-development-project-mongolia.
TA9201-MON: Gender-Responsive Sector and Local Development Policies and Actions Project Number 50093-001	2016		The project will support capacity strengthening of the national gender machinery to implement the Gender Equality Law at national, aimag, and soum levels by promoting gender equality in the political, legal, economic, social and cultural spheres, and family relations. ADB. 2022. Gender-Responsive Sector and Local Development Policies and Actions. Infographic. https://www.adb.org/news/infographics/gender-responsive-sector-local-development-policies-actions.

Legend: = Agriculture, Natural Resources, and Rural Development

 = Public Sector Management

 = Multisector

TA = technical assistance.

[a] ADB has temporarily placed on hold all sovereign project disbursements and new contracts since 1 February 2021.

Source: Authors.

C. Project Results, Photo Essays, ADB Blogs, Development Asia Case Study Articles, and Publications

Project Name	Approval Year	Sector	Project Description and Japanese Visibility/ Collaboration
Project Grants			
G9216-CAM: Agricultural Value Chain Competitiveness and Safety Enhancement Project	**2020**		The project will strengthen the value chains of competitive agricultural products and native chicken in the provinces of Kampong Cham, Kampong Thom, Oddar Meanchey, Preah Vihear, Siem Reap, and Tboung Khmum by (i) facilitating access to credit for agro-enterprises and agricultural cooperatives; (ii) promoting viable market links among agro-enterprises and agricultural cooperatives and enhance food safety and quality; and (iii) improving farm-to-market connectivity. ADB. Partnership Report 2020: Improving Value Chains to Boost Agriculture. https://www.adb.org/multimedia/partnership-report2020/stories/improving-value-chains-to-boost-agriculture/
G9198-MON: Combating Domestic Violence Against Women and Children/ G9221-MON: Combating Domestic Violence Against Women and Children-Additional Financing	**2018**		The project will strengthen quality of and access to prevention and multidisciplinary response to domestic violence by (i) delivering multidisciplinary response and livelihood assistance services to domestic violence survivors; (ii) improving capacity of key officials and staff responsible for protection and rehabilitation services; and (iii) improving behavior of key stakeholders on prevention, reporting, and protection of survivors. Turning Mongolia Orange: Behavior Change Communication Against Domestic Violence. Asian Development Blog. https://blogs.adb.org/blog/turning-mongolia-orange-behavior-change-communication-against-domestic-violence. ADB. Partnership Report 2019: Support for Survivors of Domestic Violence. https://www.adb.org/multimedia/partnership-report2019/stories/support-for-survivors-of-domestic-violence/.

Project Name	Approval Year	Sector	Project Description and Japanese Visibility/ Collaboration
G9196-IND: Enabling and Skilling Communities for Sustainable Water Services in West Bengal	2018		The project will provide safe and sustainable drinking water as per the standards set by the Government of India to over 1.65 million people in the arsenic, fluoride, and salinity-affected selected areas of Bankura, North 24 Parganas, and Purba Medinipur districts of West Bengal (project districts). It will introduce an innovative and sustainable institutional framework and advanced technology for smart water management to enable efficient service delivery in project districts. ADB. 2018. ADB Bringing Safe, Sustainable Drinking Water Service to 1.65 Million in India's West Bengal State. News release. https://www.adb.org/news/adb-bringing-safe-sustainable-drinking-water-service-165-million-indias-west-bengal-state.
G9195-MLD: Greater Male Environmental Improvement and Waste Management Project	2018		The project will establish a sustainable solid waste management system in the Greater Male capital region and its inhabited outer islands by (i) establishing a modern waste collection, transfer, and disposal system; (ii) improving community-based outer island waste management systems; (iii) building institutional capacity for sustainable services delivery; and (iv) raising public awareness in 3R behaviors. Physical and nonphysical investments are designed to curb climate change and disaster impacts while creating a cleaner environment in Maldives, one of the world's lowest-lying nations. ADB. 2020. A Clean Future for the Maldives. Photo Essay. https://www.adb.org/news/photo-essays/clean-future-maldives.
G9193-SRI: Demonstrating Innovative Approaches for Private Sector and Women Empowerment in Technical and Vocational Education and Training in Sri Lanka	2018		The project, attached to the Skills Sector Development Program (2014–2020), will build an efficient skills development system to meet labor market demand. Development Asia. 2019. Enhancing Work Skills of Young People in Sri Lanka. Case Study. https://development.asia/case-study/enhancing-work-skills-young-people-sri-lanka. Hayashi, R. 2017. Trial and Error with Digital Technology in Sri Lanka. Asian Development Blog. Manila: ADB. https://blogs.adb.org/blog/trial-and-error-digital-technology-sri-lanka.
G9188-TAJ: Water Resources Management in the Pyanj River Basin Project	2016		The Water Resources Management in the Pyanj River Basin (PRB) project will improve institutional and physical capacities of water resources management system in PRB of southern Tajikistan, to increase agricultural water productivity, by (i) establishing a PRB organization, a council, and a joint PRB committee, and developing a PRB management plan; (ii) modernizing and climate-proofing the Chubek Irrigation System; and (iii) improving farm and water use management capacities. ADB. Partnership Report 2019: Improving River Basin Management. https://www.adb.org/multimedia/partnership-report2019/stories/improving-river-basin-management-in-the-pyanj/.

Project Name	Approval Year	Sector	Project Description and Japanese Visibility/ Collaboration
G9183-MON: Integrated Livelihoods Improvement and Sustainable Tourism in Khuvsgul Lake National Park	2015		The project will support local livelihoods through improved capacity for sustainable tourism and subsistence activities, improved waste management services, and the establishment of grazing zones for herder groups. Bezuijen, M. R. 2019. Blue Skies and Green Steppe – Developing Sustainable Tourism in Mongolia. Asian Development Blog. Manila: ADB. https://blogs.adb.org/blog/blue-skies-and-green-steppe-developing-sustainable-tourism-mongolia.
G9182-MON: Improving School Dormitory Environment for Primary Students in Western Region	2015		The project will improve physical dormitory environment and capacity to deliver services in three aimags of the western region, including development of policy and regulatory frameworks to achieve these improvements. Maruyama, A. et al. 2019. Impact Evaluation Baseline Survey of School Dormitory Environment in Mongolia. Manila: ADB. https://www.adb.org/sites/default/files/publication/546896/survey-school-dormitory-primary-students-mongolia.pdf. Tayler, K. and A. Maruyama. 2020. Improving Water, Sanitation, and Hygiene in Schools - A Guide for Practicioners and Policy Makers in Mongolia. Manila: ADB. https://www.adb.org/sites/default/files/publication/603441/water-sanitation-hygiene-schools-mongolia.pdf.
G9180-NEP: Disaster Risk Reduction and Livelihood Restoration for Earthquake-affected Communities	2015		The project will improve equity and enhance social inclusion in the earthquake-affected districts and improve disaster preparedness and resilience of earthquake-affected communities by (i) constructing/rebuilding model disaster-resilient schools; (ii) providing a microcredit facility for livelihood restoration to small farmer cooperatives; and (iii) strengthening DRM capacity of the affected communities. ADB. 2017. Building Schools Better in Nepal. Project Result/ Case Study. https://www.adb.org/results/building-schools-better-nepal. ADB. 2020. Five Years after the Nepal Earthquake – Building Back Better Schools for a Safer Future. Project Result/Case Study. https://www.adb.org/results/five-years-after-nepal-earthquake-building-back-better-schools-safer-future. Yokoyama, K. 2015. New Grant to Rebuild Schools, Provide Micro Loans after Nepal Earthquake. Asian Development Blog. Manila: ADB. https://blogs.adb.org/blog/new-grant-rebuild-schools-provide-micro-loans-after-nepal-earthquake. Yokoyama, K. 2016. We Must Build Capacity, Speed Up Nepal Earthquake Reconstruction. Asian Development Blog. https://blogs.adb.org/blog/we-must-build-capacity-speed-nepal-earthquake-reconstruction. Ozaki, M. 2019. Microfinance Can Be a Powerful Force in Disaster Recovery. Asian Development Blog. https://blogs.adb.org/blog/microfinance-can-be-powerful-force-disaster-recovery.

Project Name	Approval Year	Sector	Project Description and Japanese Visibility/ Collaboration
G9176-MYA: Greater Mekong Subregion Capacity Building for HIV/AIDS Prevention[a]	2013		The project contributed toward achieving the Millennium Development Goal targets by reversing/managing the spread of HIV/AIDS in Myanmar by increasing the coverage and quality of information and services (prevention, treatment, and care) for targeted populations along and near the economic corridors. ADB. 2014. Greater Mobility in Myanmar Raises Risks of Communicable Disease Contagion. https://www.adb.org/news/features/greater-mobility-myanmar-raises-risks-communicable-disease-contagion.
G9175-PHI: Emergency Assistance and Early Recovery for Poor Municipalities Affected by Typhoon Yolanda	2013		The project will mitigate the adverse social and economic impacts on the poor resulting from Typhoon Yolanda in the Eastern Visayas through (i) restoring local government unit infrastructure and providing access to emergency employment and livelihood support; (ii) providing basic emergency maternal and child health care services; (iii) and improving resilience to future disasters and effective project management, coordination, monitoring, and reporting. ADB. 2014. Classrooms of Hope: Typhoon Yolanda One Year On. https://www.adb.org/results/classrooms-hope-typhoon-yolanda-one-year. ADB. 2015. Young Survivors Graduate from School after Typhoon Yolanda. Photo Essay. https://www.adb.org/news/photo-essays/young-survivors-graduate-school-after-typhoon-yolanda. ADB. 2014. Yolanda Anniversary Highlights Progress, And Need For Resilient Reconstruction. News Release. https://www.adb.org/news/yolanda-anniversary-highlights-progress-and-need-resilient-reconstruction. ADB. Typhoon Haiyan: A Tale of Relief and Recovery. https://adb.exposure.co/typhoon-yolanda. ADB. 2014. Yolanda, One Year Later: From Relief to Reconstruction - Stephen Groff. Op-Ed/Opinion. https://www.adb.org/news/op-ed/yolanda-one-year-later-relief-reconstruction-stephen-groff. ADB. 2014. Typhoon Yolanda (Haiyan): Asian Development Bank Assistance. https://www.adb.org/publications/typhoon-yolanda-haiyan-asian-development-bank-assistance.

Project Name	Approval Year	Sector	Project Description and Japanese Visibility/ Collaboration
G9174-MYA: Enhancing Rural Livelihoods and Incomes[a]	2013		The project provided one consolidated investment grant of $12 million to target four diverse geographic (and agro-ecological) regions in Myanmar to implement different interventions based on topography, agricultural production systems, and natural resource management regimes focusing on two interrelated sets of activities: (i) improvements and upgrades of social and productive infrastructure; and (ii) improvement of capacities of communities and project line agencies at the local and state levels, and to a lesser degree at the central levels. ADB. 2013. Community-Driven Development in Myanmar. Photo Essay. https://www.adb.org/news/photo-essays/community-driven-development-myanmar.
G9173-REG: GMS: Livelihood Support for Corridor Towns	2013		The project will pilot a poverty reduction approach in the Greater Mekong Subregion using a market development approach intended to complement the urban infrastructure investments under three ADB loan projects by helping poor informal traders enhance their locally produced products and provide aesthetically attractive, environmentally sound, socially inclusive, and gender-responsive trade centers to market these products. Development Asia. 2019. Increasing Economic Activities through Night Markets. Case Study. https://development.asia/case-study/increasing-economic-activities-through-night-markets.
G9172-BAN: Pilot Project on Weather Index-based Crop Insurance	2013		The project will develop and implement weather index-based crop insurance in Bangladesh as an adaptation tool to reduce the climate variability and extreme weather vulnerability of the agriculture sector, especially impacting small farm households. Arup Kumar Chatterjee, A. K. 2018. Crop Insurance Lessons from My Field Trip to Rajshahi. Asian Development Blog. Manila: ADB. https://blogs.adb.org/blog/crop-insurance-lessons-my-field-trip-rajshahi
G9166-SAM: Community Sanitation Project	2012		The project will provide vulnerable households sustainable access to better sanitation in targeted regions of Samoa by establishing and piloting an innovative delivery method and institutional arrangements for providing subsidized sanitation infrastructure to low-income households. ADB. 2017. Villages in Samoa Improve Sanitation to Stay Healthy. Project Result/Case Study. https://www.adb.org/results/villages-samoa-improve-sanitation-stay-healthy.

Project Name	Approval Year	Sector	Project Description and Japanese Visibility/Collaboration
G9162-PHI: Promoting Partnership and Innovations in Poor and Underserved Communities	2012		The project will pilot a viable model for strengthening strategic multisectoral partnerships to support the sustainable development of poor and underserved communities that can be replicated in the Philippines and other developing member countries of ADB through (i) piloting a program for expanding multisectoral partnerships; (ii) improving access to basic services, including economic and livelihood opportunities; (iii) enhancing capacities of residents in community development and social entrepreneurship; and (iv) establishing an effective project management, monitoring and evaluation, and reporting system. ADB. 2012. ADB, Japan Grant to Benefit Almost 6,000 Families in Laguna's Southville 7. News Release. https://www.adb.org/news/adb-japan-grant-benefit-almost-6000-families-lagunas-southville-7. ADB. 2016. Making Resettlement Work through Partnerships. Case Study. Manila: ADB. https://development.asia/case-study/making-resettlement-work-through-partnerships.
G9160-REG: Developing Sustainable Alternative Livelihoods in Coastal Fishing Communities in the Coral Triangle: Indonesia and Philippines	2011		The project will raise the income levels of the poor coastal communities in Berau, East Kalimantan, Indonesia and Balabac, Palawan, Philippines by pilot-testing support mechanisms for sustainable livelihoods that will involve women and indigenous peoples through (i) social preparation activities; and (ii) livelihood development, implementation, and training/capacity building. ADB. Partnership Report 2019: Securing Sustainable Income while Protecting the Environment. https://www.adb.org/multimedia/partnership-report2019/stories/securing-sustainable-incomes-while-protecting-the-environment/.
G9152-MON: Promoting Inclusive Financial Services for the Poor	2010		The project will increase the number of poor and vulnerable nonpoor (male and female) who become members of savings and credit cooperatives through improving the basic understanding of household financial management and available financial services with the use of TV drama series. Enkhbold, E. 2016. TV Drama Promotes Financial Education in Mongolia. Asian Development Blog. Manila: ADB. https://blogs.adb.org/author/enerelt-enkhbold.
G9136-MON: Protecting the Health Status of the Poor during Financial Crisis	2009		The project will ensure that the poor have free access to essential health services to mitigate the impact of the financial crisis through a medicard program that uses existing institutional arrangements of the health insurance system to reimburse participating facilities. Development Asia. 2020. How Crisis Interventions Can Help Develop Long-Term Health System Reforms. Manila: ADB. https://development.asia/insight/how-crisis-interventions-can-help-develop-long-term-health-system-reforms.

Project Name	Approval Year	Sector	Project Description and Japanese Visibility/Collaboration
G9135-NEP: Establishing Women and Services Centers	2009		The project will reduce vulnerability and helplessness of women and children in five rural districts of Nepal by providing professional and coordinated protection and assistance to female and child victims of crimes such as rape, domestic violence, polygamy, allegations of witchcraft, child abuse, child marriage, and trafficking. ADB. 2013. Empowering Women in Bangladesh, Nepal, and the Philippines. Project Result/Case Study. https://www.adb.org/results/empowering-women-bangladesh-nepal-and-philippines. ADB. 2019. Police and Community Partnership in Nepal Tackling Violence Against Women. Project Result/Case Study. https://www.adb.org/results/police-and-community-partnership-nepal-tackling-violence-against-women. ADB. Safer Homes and Communities for Women and Children. https://www.adb.org/multimedia/donor-report2018/our-stories/safer-homes-communities-women-and-children.html.
G9111-TAJ: Sustainable Access for Isolated Rural Communities	2007		The project will improve over 14 km of rural roads connecting nearby communities to the bridge, which is part of ADB's ongoing work to build a 227 m bridge and just over 1 km of road leading up to the bridge. ADB. 2013. Tajikistan Transport: Surhob River Bridge Saves Lives. Project Result/Case Study. https://www.adb.org/results/tajikistan-transport-surhob-river-bridge-saves-lives. ADB. 2013. Bridge Transforms Lives of Isolated Villagers in Tajikistan. Photo Essay. https://www.adb.org/news/photo-essays/bridge-transforms-lives-isolated-villagers-tajikistan.
G9103-BHU: Rural Skills Development Project	2007		The project will address an acute shortage of trained personnel at all skill levels and improve the efficiency and productivity of public and private agencies, in support of ADB–Government of Bhutan's partnership on vocational training programs. ADB. 2010. Promoting Vocational Training in Bhutan. Project Result/Case Study. https://www.adb.org/results/promoting-vocational-training-bhutan.

Project Name	Approval Year	Sector	Project Description and Japanese Visibility/ Collaboration
G9101-NEP: Improving the Livelihood of Poor Farmers and Disadvantaged Groups in the Eastern Development Region	2006		The project will allow the most marginalized and disadvantaged households (low caste, Dalit, ethnic minority groups, female-headed households) in four districts of the Eastern Development Region to effectively participate in and benefit from the development of the agricultural value chain through (i) high-value crop production, vegetable farming, and other income generation activities; and (ii) social mobilization and literacy and numeracy courses, capacity development and skills training, provision of seed packages, micro irrigation, and linkages to the Commercial Agriculture Development Project and its matching grant funds. ADB. 2012. Supporting Agriculture and Woman's Rights in Nepal. Project Result/Case Study. https://www.adb.org/results/supporting-agriculture-and-womans-rights-nepal.
G9081-CAM: Women's Development Centers	2005		The project will reduce poverty through increased access to services that support women's social and economic empowerment in Cambodia through (i) facilitating life skills training and advocacy support, (ii) promoting micro and small entrepreneurship development and support through adequate information, facilitation of access to credit, and enabling links to various organizations and resources, and (iii) building capacity of institutions that promote women-friendly entrepreneurial environments. ADB. 2013. Cambodia Gender: Vocational Skills Training Uplifts Women. Project Result/Case Study. https://www.adb.org/results/cambodia-gender-vocational-skills-training-uplifts-women, Schelzig, K. 2013. Cambodia's Rural Women Beating Poverty with Partnerships. Asian Development Blog. Manila: ADB. https://blogs.adb.org/blog/cambodia-s-rural-women-beating-poverty-partnerships.

Project Name	Approval Year	Sector	Project Description and Japanese Visibility/ Collaboration
G9045-SRI: Power Fund for the Poor **G9077-SRI: Post-Tsunami Utility Connections to the Poor** *(Information on both projects, approved in 2004 (G9045) and 2005 (G9077), are no longer on the adb.org website)*	2004	⚡	The projects, attached to the Sri Lanka Power Sector Development program loan, will (i) establish an independent regulatory and tariff-setting mechanism; (ii) enhance sector efficiency by introducing competition and commercialization; and (iii) encourage private sector participation in the sector by developing an enabling, transparent business environment. The program loan will also address the drain on national resources arising from the financial deterioration of the state-owned utility, Ceylon Electricity Board. The accompanying grant projects (Power Fund for the Poor and Post-Tsunami Utility Connections for the Poor) will ensure that the poor and marginalized—including households headed by females—can access electricity services. ADB. 2012. Sri Lanka: Power Sector Development Program Loan 1929/1930-2010. Project Result/Case Study. https://www.adb.org/results/sri-lanka-power-sector-development-program-loan-19291930-2010. ADB. 2010. Gender Equality Results Case Studies: Sri Lanka. Manila. https://www.adb.org/sites/default/files/publication/28746/gender-case-study-sri.pdf.
G9042-PHI: Renewable Energy and Livelihood Development for the Poor in Negros Occidental	2004	⚡	The project will provide and utilize the renewable energy supply to promote sustainable livelihood systems for poor local communities in off-grid areas of the Philippines within the framework of public–private–civil society partnership. ADB. 2010. The Power of the River. Project Result/Case Study. https://www.adb.org/results/power-river.
Technical Assistance			
TA6854-REG: Improving Water Security and Resilience through Digitalization – Improving Water Security and Resilience through Digitalization (Subproject 2)	2021	🚰	The TA will support the achievement of the TA cluster outcome of resilient investments and policies in the water sector by raising the awareness and improving the capacity of selected municipal and village governing bodies, utilities, or water resource management entities, or other water-related organizations and agencies on resilience. ADB. 2021. ARe yoU Water Resilient? A Bottom-Up Initiative for Water Resilience in Asia and the Pacific. https://www.adb.org/sites/default/files/publication/748211/bottom-water-resilience-asia-pacific.pdf.
TA6536-REG: Nowcasting and Disasters: Impact- Based Forecasting and Socioeconomic Monitoring	2020	🏢	The knowledge and support TA will establish a monitoring platform to assess in near-real time the economic impacts of disasters, and trace social, environmental, and other indicators of relevance. ADB. Partnership 2020: Outpacing Disasters and Pandemics to Support Economic Resilience. https://www.adb.org/multimedia/partnership-report2020/stories/outpacing-disasters-pandemics-to-support-economic-resilience/.

Project Name	Approval Year	Sector	Project Description and Japanese Visibility/ Collaboration
TA 9595-IND: Madhya Pradesh Skills Development Project	2018		The TA will assist the Government of Madhya Pradesh in transforming its technical and vocational education and training system to create a skilled workforce that meets the evolving development needs of the state by establishing a new advanced institute of international standards to introduce high-quality, technology-oriented skills training for the state's priority sectors, modernizing 10 major industrial training institutes with upgraded training infrastructure and curricula to impart quality, industry-relevant skills. ADB. 2018. ADB Supports India's First TVET Skills Park to Boost Employability in Madhya Pradesh. News Release. https://www.adb.org/news/adb-supports-indias-first-tvet-skills-park-boost-employability-madhya-pradesh.
TA9459-UZB: Power Sector Reform and Sustainability Support Program	2017		The TA, attached to the investment project that will construct two units of 450 MW energy-efficient combined cycle gas turbines at the Talimarjan Thermal Power Plant located in Kashkadarya region, will improve corporate governance, final operation, and performance, and enhance institutional capacity contributing to energy saving, greenhouse gas emission reduction, and reliable power supply in Uzbekistan. Abbasov, R. 2018. Uzbekistan – From Vertically Integrated Electricity Utility to Energy Hub of Central Asia. Asian Development Blog. Manila: ADB. https://blogs.adb.org/blog/uzbekistan-vertically-integrated-electricity-utility-energy-hub-central-asia.
TA9346-NEP: South Asia Subregional Economic Cooperation Customs Reform and Modernization for Trade Facilitation	2017		The South Asia Subregional Economic Cooperation Customs Reform and Modernization for Trade Facilitation Program will contribute to Nepal's national goals of promoting and diversifying exports, and help the country fulfill its commitments to the Trade Facilitation Agreement of the World Trade Organization and related international standards on customs. Abdou, M., R. Butiong, U. Kumar, B. Shepherd. 2019. Borders Without Barriers: Facilitating Trade in SASEC Countries. Manila: ADB. https://www.adb.org/sites/default/files/publication/541971/borders-without-barriers-facilitating-trade-sasec.pdf.
TA9314-MYA: Greater Mekong Subregion East-West Economic Corridor Highway Development[a]	2017		The TA aimed to conduct a project feasibility study to develop an arterial highway between Bago and Kyaikto of about 75 km, along the Greater Mekong Subregion East–West Economic Corridor. Thomas, E. 2015. Working in Conflict-Affected Areas – The Myanmar Experience. Asian Development Blog. Manila: ADB. https://blogs.adb.org/blog/working-conflict-affected-areas-myanmar-experience.

Project Name	Approval Year	Sector	Project Description and Japanese Visibility/Collaboration
TA9256-UZB: Skills Strategies for Industrial Modernization and Inclusive Growth	2016		The TA will formulate a framework for a more effective and relevant skills development system that supports industrial modernization and inclusive growth by (i) identifying and analyzing skills demand and supply in Navoi region, Angren district of Tashkent region, and Andijan region; (ii) establishing a skills monitoring system to address emerging jobs designed and pilot program; and (iii) identifying and assessing the possible reform and program design options to improve the skills development system. Martinez, C. 2017. Boosting Competitiveness through Skills Development in Uzbekistan. Asian Development Blog. Manila: ADB. https://blogs.adb.org/blog/boosting-competitiveness-through-skills-development-uzbekistan.
TA9201-MON: Gender-Responsive Sectoral and Local Development Policies and Actions	2016		The TA will support the strengthening of capacity of the national gender machinery to implement the Gender Equality Law at national, aimag, and soum levels through promotion of gender equality in the political, legal, economic, social, and cultural spheres, and family relations. Development Asia. 2019. Communication Strategies to Enforce Gender Equality Legislation in Mongolia. Case Study. Manila: ADB. https://development.asia/case-study/communication-strategies-enforce-gender-equality-legislation-mongolia.
TA9170-REG: Promoting Smart Systems in ADB's Future Cities Program	2016		The regional research and development TA will contribute to promoting smart infrastructure and systems in selected cities under the Future Cities Program of ADB, with particular emphasis on pro-poor support, facilitating positive steps toward sustainable and livable cities, and knowledge solutions by identifying smart solutions that could lead to the preparation of relevant investment projects where ADB could provide further financing assistance. Roño, C. A. 2018. Creating Open, Honest Government Through Blockchain. Asian Development Blog. Manila: ADB. https://blogs.adb.org/blog/creating-open-honest-government-through-blockchain.

Project Name	Approval Year	Sector	Project Description and Japanese Visibility/ Collaboration
TA9111-REG: Strengthening Developing Member Countries' Capacity in Elderly Care	2016		The TA will improve strategic planning and policy development in elderly care through (i) preparation of six country diagnostic studies to cover policy and regulatory frameworks, institutional arrangements and capacity, needs of older people and service provider assessments, human resources (constraints and development), existing programs and coverage, and financing; (ii) a capacity building framework prepared based on the findings of the country diagnostic studies and feedback from earlier national consultations with a wide range of stakeholders; and (iii) knowledge sharing and networking systems developed with establishment of partnerships with centers of excellence. Kumar, U. 2020. Charting Sri Lanka's Aging Population. Asian Development Blog. Manila: ADB. https://blogs.adb.org/blog/charting-sri-lankas-aging-population. ADB. 2019. Growing Old Before Becoming Rich: Challenges of an Aging Population in Sri Lanka. Manila. https://www.adb.org/sites/default/files/publication/557446/aging-population-sri-lanka.pdf.
TA9080-SRI: Cluster Development and Small and Medium-Sized Enterprise Finance Innovation	2016		The TA will develop innovative financial schemes for small and medium-sized enterprises (SMEs) and promoting export-oriented cluster development and attached to a credit line for 10 participating financial institutions targeting SMEs, including SMEs that are led by women, are first-time borrowers, do not sufficient collateral, and are outside of Colombo. ADB. Partnership Report 2019: Access to Credit Empowers Sri Lankan Women. https://www.adb.org/multimedia/partnership-report2019/stories/access-to-credit-empowers-sri-lankan-women/.
TA9016-BHU: Decentralized Coordination and Partnership for Gender Equality Results	2015		The TA will help the poor, particularly women, gain access to government services and resources by creating greater awareness within government agencies of gender equality concerns. Mercer-Blackman, V. 2019. Estimating the Value of Women's Unpaid Work in Asia's Homes. Asian Development Blog. Manila: ADB. https://blogs.adb.org/blog/estimating-value-women-s-unpaid-work-asia-s-homes.

Project Name	Approval Year	Sector	Project Description and Japanese Visibility/Collaboration
TA8881-REG: Capacity Building for Developing Qualification Frameworks under the Mutual Recognition Agreements (MRAs) to Support Association of Southeast Asian Nations Economic Community (AEC) by 2015 and Beyond (2015)	2015		The TA will support implementation of the MRAs and, more broadly, the goals of the AEC, especially its first pillar (i) involving free skill mobility; (ii) increasing the competitiveness and productivity of countries and the region, thereby supporting the second generation of regional cooperation and integration; (iii) harmonizing standards related to skill mobility across countries in the region; and (iv) promoting trade and investment by facilitating skill mobility. Édes, B. 2019. Migration in Asia: Where Is Everybody Going? Asian Development Blog. Manila: ADB. https://blogs.adb.org/blog/migration-asia-where-everybody-going. Takenaka, A. K. and E. Suan. 2019. Promoting Skilled Labor Mobility and Migration in Southeast Asia. Asian Development Blog. Manila: ADB. https://blogs.adb.org/blog/promoting-skilled-labor-mobility-and-migration-southeast-asia. Sasiwimon Warunsiri Paweenawat, S. W. and J. Vechbanyongratana. 2020. Lessons We Can Learn from Thai Engineers. Asian Development Blog. Manila: ADB. https://blogs.adb.org/blog/lessons-we-can-learn-thai-engineers. Gentile, E., ed. 2019. *Skilled Labor Mobility and Migration: Challenges and Opportunities for the ASEAN Economic Community*. London: ADB/Edward Elgar Publishing. https://www.adb.org/sites/default/files/publication/517601/skilled-labor-mobility-migration-asean.pdf. Papademetriou, D. G., G. Sugiyarto, D. R. Mendoza, and B. Salant. 2015. Achieving Skill Mobility in the ASEAN Economic Community: Challenges, Opportunities, and Policy Implications. Manila: ADB. https://www.adb.org/sites/default/files/publication/178816/skill-mobility-asean.pdf.
TA8850-MON: Ensuring Inclusiveness and Service Delivery for Persons with Disabilities	2014		The TA will support the Government of Mongolia in addressing a major social problem by ensuring inclusiveness and delivery of services for persons with disabilities in Ulaanbaatar and at the aimag (province) level through access to employment and increase their autonomy and contribution to the economy and society in general. ADB. 2019. *Living with Disability in Mongolia: Progress toward Inclusion*. Manila. https://www.adb.org/sites/default/files/publication/548006/living-disability-mongolia.pdf.

Project Name	Approval Year	Sector	Project Description and Japanese Visibility/ Collaboration
TA 8803-BAN: Strengthening Monitoring and Enforcement in the Meghna River for Dhaka's Sustainable Water Supply	2014		The TA will ensure sustainable water supply from Meghna River to Dhaka City by strengthening government capacity for water quality monitoring and enforcing laws for maintaining the river's water quality through (i) a monitoring and reporting system, including water pollution mapping; (ii) piloting an incentive or reward system for pollution control; (iii) identifying ecologically critical areas and preparing for designation; and (iv) conducting training. Chowdhury, F. J., Z. U. Ahmad, and H. Aalderink. 2019. *Protecting the Meghna River: A Sustainable Water Resource for Dhaka*. Manila: ADB. https://www.adb.org/sites/default/files/publication/519666/meghna-river-sustainable-water-resource-dhaka.pdf.
TA8802-MON: Strategic Planning for Peatlands	2014		The TA will increase the capacity of the Ministry of Environment and Green Development to (i) formulate a clear guiding framework in addressing the peatland restoration and management issues such as climate change, ecosystem, and water management issues; and (ii) develop opportunities for improved livelihoods for communities dependent on or associated with peatlands. ADB. 2018. Mongolia Battles to Save its Peatlands, and a Nomadic Way of Life. Project Result/Case Study. https://www.adb.org/results/mongolia-battles-save-its-peatlands-and-nomadic-way-life.
TA8623-BHU: Adapting to Climate Change through Integrated Water Resources Management	2014		The capacity development TA will support the National Environment Commission and other relevant government agencies to implement specific elements of the 2011 Water Act and related Water Regulation (to be approved) and promote IWRM to facilitate effective river basin management and strengthen resilience to current variability and anticipated impacts of future climate change. Development Asia. 2019. Taking a Sustainable and Holistic Approach to Water Resources Management. Case Study. Manila: ADB. https://development.asia/case-study/taking-sustainable-and-holistic-approach-water-resources-management. ADB. Bhutan: Managing Water Resources, Readying for Climate Change. https://www.adb.org/multimedia/donor-report2018/our-stories/managing-water-resources-readying-climate-change.html.

Project Name	Approval Year	Sector	Project Description and Japanese Visibility/ Collaboration
TA8369-REG: Innovative Data Collection Methods for Agricultural and Rural Statistics	2013		The TA will promote the use of satellite-based technology in formulating and monitoring food security policies by (i) developing customized software applications and methodology to estimate paddy rice cultivation area and crop production based on satellite data and data obtained through crop-cutting experiments at a provincial level; (ii) training counterpart staff in the four pilot countries; and (iii) developing an online training program on the use of satellite data for agricultural and rural statistics. Rao, L. N. and P. Lapitan. 2016. The Curious Case of Area Measurement in Surveys (I). Asian Development Blog. Manila: ADB. https://blogs.adb.org/blog/curious-case-area-measurement-surveys-i. Lapitan, P. and A. C. D. Durante. 2019. Harvesting the Good Data that Asia's Farmers Need. Asian Development Blog. Manila: ADB. https://blogs.adb.org/blog/harvesting-good-data-asia-s-farmers-need. Durante, A. C., P. Lapitan, D. Megill, and L. N. Rao. 2018. Improving Paddy Rice Statistics Using Area Sampling Frame Technique. *ADB Economics Working Paper Series*. No. 565. Manila: ADB. https://www.adb.org/sites/default/files/publication/468871/ewp-565-improving-paddy-rice-statistics.pdf.
TA8224-INO: Improving Access to Finance in Aceh and North Sumatra	2012		The TA will support the governments of Aceh and North Sumatra in developing integrated support to improve access to finance by (i) supporting capacity enhancement of said governments; (ii) assisting local banks to develop new microfinance products, including Grameen-type products and suitable follow-on products; and (iii) supporting the Government of Aceh to develop sustainable Local Guarantee Cooperation to facilitate credit access of feasible borrowers. ADB. 2017. Small Loans Help Bring in the Big Fish in Indonesia. Project Result/Case Study. https://www.adb.org/results/small-loans-help-bring-big-fish-indonesia.
TA7843-INO: Strengthening Sanitation Planning and Efficiency Improvement	2011		The TA will improve access to service delivery and healthy livelihoods for the poor, near poor, and women in the project communities through (i) strengthening capacity for community planning and development; (ii) improving rural basic infrastructure through community development grants; and (iii) improving sanitation services through neighborhood development grants. Development Asia. 2018. Mainstreaming Gender in Urban Sanitation and Rural Infrastructure Projects. Case Study. Manila: ADB. https://development.asia/case-study/mainstreaming-gender-urban-sanitation-and-rural-infrastructure-projects. Development Asia. 2018. Empowering Women through a Community-Driven Project. Manila: ADB. https://development.asia/insight/empowering-women-through-community-driven-project.

Project Name	Approval Year	Sector	Project Description and Japanese Visibility/ Collaboration
TA7733-PHI: Support for Social Protection Reform	2010		The policy advisory TA will support the ongoing social protection reform of the Government of the Philippines, including convergence in the social protection sector and rationalization of the overall social protection portfolio by (i) providing support to formulate and implement an action plan for rationalization and coordination of existing social protection programs; and (ii) supporting the establishment of a "referral system" for the poorest population, linked to the newly established national household targeting system. Development Asia. 2016. Expanding Cash Grant Systems. Policy Brief. Manila: ADB. https://development.asia/policy-brief/expanding-cash-grant-systems.
TA7591-MON: Ulaanbaatar Water and Sanitation Services and Planning Improvement	2010		The TA will identify potential areas for ADB lending in urban services and provide key policy recommendations to improve services and regulations in the planning, delivery, and coverage of municipal infrastructure services by focusing on water and sanitation services and ger areas. ADB. Mongolia: Water and Sanitation in City Master Planning. https://www.adb.org/multimedia/donor-report2018/our-stories/water-sanitation-city-master-planning.html. Development Asia. 2019. Plugging In Unplanned Settlements in a City Master Plan. Case Study. Manila: ADB. https://development.asia/case-study/plugging-unplanned-settlements-city-master-plan.

Legend: = Agriculture, Natural Resources, and Rural Development   = Industry and Trade

= Education   = Multisector

= Energy   = Public Sector Management

= Finance   = Transport

= Health   = Water and Other Urban Infrastructure and Services

DRM = disaster risk management, km = kilometer, TA = technical assistance.
a   ADB has temporarily placed on hold all sovereign project disbursements and new contracts since 1 February 2021.
Source: Authors.

JFPR Frequently Asked Questions

A. General

Q1: What happens to an ongoing JFPR project that is using the old name? Do we need to change it to the new name and apply this to all its records?

A1: Yes. A memo dated 10 January 2022 was sent to all user departments on the letter template to be issued to executing agencies (EAs)/implementing agencies (IAs) and other stakeholders of ongoing JFPR projects on the name change. Further, JFPR's records in ADB internal systems have been updated to the new name.

Q2: Under the new JFPR, will there be maximum country ceilings? How about priority area budget ceilings?

A2: There is no country ceiling but SDPF will manage the distribution balance. For the priority areas, the Government of Japan (GOJ) will decide on completion and consultation of the proposal list.

Q3: Is it possible to obtain a waiver for a JFPR project grant to exclude government engagement and to have it processed and later implemented through a civil society organization (CSO)/ nongovernment organization (NGO) or international consultant as the IA and ADB as the EA (as with TA)?

A3: In exceptional cases, processing and implementation of a JFPR project grant through a CSO/NGO excluding the government may be feasible subject to consultation with and endorsement by GOJ.

Q4: International travel is ineligible for expenses: are there exemptions to this provision, particularly if justification is provided in terms of participation in an international/regional workshop?

A4: For clarity, international travel of civil servants is ineligible. On a case-by-case basis, such expenditure may exceptionally be accepted depending on the justification, subject to approval by GOJ (e.g., if it will enhance the Japanese visibility aspect of the project, etc.).

Q5: Are there any specific guidelines regarding cofinancing JFPR funds with other funding sources?

A5: Clear demarcation of support among all funding sources including JFPR should be ensured, as well as no comingling of funds.

Q6: Will the new JFPR guidelines affect projects approved prior to 2022?

A6: The new JFPR Implementation Guidelines will be applied to ongoing JFPR projects (i.e., those approved prior to 2022).

Q7: Is retroactive financing under a project grant allowed under the new JFPR?

A7: Yes. In principle, JFPR projects will be processed and implemented in accordance with ADB's relevant policies and guidelines unless specific provisions are stipulated in the JFPR Implementation Guidelines.

Q8: Is it a requirement that proposals for submission be included in the Country Partnership Strategy (CPS) or the Indicative Country Pipeline and Monitoring (ICPM) report?

A8: JFPR projects should be aligned with the developing member country development agenda as well as ADB strategies. As such, it is preferred that their proposals be included in the CPS or ICPM report.

Q9: Does the new JFPR prioritize the TRTA attached to investment loans?

A9: No. The new JFPR supports all TA types as long as they are eligible under the new priority areas.

Q10: Are JFPR projects eligible under ADB's universal procurement policy?

A10: No. JFPR has issued a blanket waiver in terms of inclusion in the universal procurement policy.

B. Coordination with Sector/Thematic Groups

Q11: What will happen to ongoing proposals whose concepts were cleared using the old JFPR process? Do they need to consult with STGs before they proceed with proposal submission?

A11: Yes. Project teams should consult with the relevant STGs to ensure the proposal is eligible under the new JFPR's priorities. Moreover, the STG focal should be included as a peer reviewer.

Q12: How does coordination with the STGs work for pipeline creation? Should project officers approach the STGs? Or will the STGs solicit the list from user departments? What is the timeline for such submissions from user departments?

A12: User departments will coordinate with relevant STGs on the indicative list of potential projects on a semiannual basis (i.e., June and December) to be provided to the SDPF–JFPR Team and submitted to GOJ. If needed, the SDPF-JFPR Team will facilitate the process to prepare the indicative list, including initiating a call for proposals for STGs and user departments.

Q13: The priority areas are cross-cutting; if a proposal is eligible in two or more of the priority areas (e.g., QII + CC/DRM), who should we consult? Who decides which priority area to place it in?

A13: It depends on the components. For example, if the main objective is climate change and disaster risk management (CC/DRM), consultation with SDCC will suffice. To ensure smooth processing, it is encouraged that the proposal come under one priority area only. On the other hand, if both QII and CC/DRM are main objectives, project teams should consult both relevant STGs prior to concept submission.

Q14: If our proposal is not on the list, can we still propose and submit to JFPR?

A14: A proposal that is not on the list can still be accommodated. Once confirmed as eligible by the relevant STGs, such a proposal will be added to the list even after its submission to GOJ (the list is a living document).

Q15: Is consultation with STGs required under PR support?

A15: Coordination with STGs under PR support is not required under the JFPR process but project teams may still consult with STGs.

Q16: Who is the STG focal in each of the priority areas? Who should we approach?

A16: The table below shows the relevant STG per priority area.

Universal Health Coverage	Climate Change and Disaster Risk Management	Quality Infrastructure Investment	Public Finance Management
Health Sector Group	Climate Change and Disaster Risk Management Thematic Group	Governance Thematic Group (other Sector/Thematic Groups depending on the components)	Governance Thematic Group
Contacts:			
Patrick Osewe Arindam Dutta	Charlotte Benson Arghya Sinha Roy	Hyun Chang Park	Jose Luis Syquia Rachana Shrestha

Note: For Poverty Reduction support, coordinate directly with the SDPF-JFPR Team. Contact details are as of June 2022.

C. Japanese Visibility

Q17: Is it acceptable if the experts to be hired are non-Japanese nationals but from Japanese institutions? Or are Japanese nationals required? What about international development partners based in Japan?

A17: It is not a requirement that experts engaged from Japanese institutions are Japanese nationals as long as Japanese knowledge or know-how and experience are used and adopted in the project.

Q18: Will there be new requirements regarding Japanese visibility and Japan's expectations on visibility in ADB/JFPR joint initiatives?

A18: No, the same Japanese visibility requirements are expected under the new JFPR. Detailed information can be found in the Guidance Note on Japanese Visibility.

Q19: On the signing of memoranda of understanding with partner institutions/agencies, do we have to include EOJ and JICA as witnesses?

A19: Yes. EOJ and JICA officials may be invited to the signing ceremony and/or other publicity events under JFPR projects.

Q20: Is there any threshold or certain percentage for use on Japanese visibility?

A20: JFPR project grants have administrative budget support up to 3% of the total grant amount that can be used to enhance Japanese visibility, such as through the engagement of Japanese experts or knowledge products to showcase the project outputs.

D. Coordination with EOJ and JICA

Q21: For regional technical assistance (RETA), is the process of consulting with EOJ and JICA still mandatory, or are there any changes? Will it also be on a no-objection basis, or do these actors need to provide technical and strategic comments as well?

A21: Yes, this is still mandatory. For RETAs, e-mail consultation will suffice, and this works on a no-objection basis within a 2-week time frame. In the case of fundamental comments, project teams are also expected to address these.

Q22: Will it be possible for the SDPF–JFPR Team to facilitate the introduction to EOJ and JICA even before the JFPR application has been officially submitted? Is there guidance on how to approach EOJ and JICA for close coordination at an early stage?

A22: Yes, the SDPF–JFPR Team can provide EOJ and JICA contact information for the recipient countries and facilitate consultation with EOJ/JICA as needed. For more information, refer to the Guidance Note on Coordination with EOJ and JICA.

E. Processing

Q23: Is a hybrid project (i.e., project grant and TA combined) still acceptable under the new JFPR?

A23: A hybrid project is acceptable only in <u>exceptional cases</u> and provided there is strong justification why JFPR should support both modalities, such as grant activities that will complement the TA activities and vice versa. Moreover, strong Japanese visibility measures should be adopted while implementing such a project.

Q24: Can JFPR and the Japan Special Fund (JSF) support one ADB project (i.e., through a JFPR project grant and JSF TA)?

A24: Such a case is technically possible but not expected given the rationale and background to the funds.

Q25: If a TA proposal is ineligible under JFPR can it automatically be processed under JSF?

A25: It can be processed under JSF but not automatically. It will still be subject to eligibility requirements based on consistency with the JSF objectives, portfolio (country/sector balance), fund availability, etc.

Q26: Can JFPR still consider additional financing request for ongoing projects or facilities?

A26: Yes, but strong justification is required on the role and additional component/activity to be funded by JFPR, and JFPR's support should be distinct from the overall TA.

Q27: Does the $2 million limit apply to topping up an existing TA?

A27: $2 million is the maximum if the ongoing TA is funded by other sources; $1 million is the maximum amount if the ongoing TA is funded by JFPR.

Q28: Is there a deadline for proposal submission?

A28: There is no deadline for proposal submission but confirmation from the STG on the project's eligibility is required to initiate the JFPR process.

Q29: What is the new JFPR's indicative processing timeline, taking into consideration coordination with relevant STGs?

A29: JFPR's processing workflow indicates a minimum of 30 working days from the submission of the concept to SDPF (i.e., relevant STGs have confirmed its eligibility) to GOJ approval. This excludes cases when proposals are returned with comments.

Q30: In the case of unexpected processing delays from ADB's side, is there a validity period for JFPR funding?

A30: GOJ approval validity is 6 months for JFPR TA and JSF and 1 year for JFPR project grants. This may be extended upon e-mail consultation with and request to the SDPF–JFPR Team.

Q31: Can additional "seed money" be provided to attached JFPR project grants?

A31: No. Seed money is for <u>stand-alone PR project grants</u> only.

F. Implementation

Q32: ADB's implementation of JFPR project grant components is not allowed. Is there a chance that this will change?

A32: For now, this is not allowed. We will inform the user departments if there are changes to this provision.

Q33: Is there a specific schedule to follow to report the accomplishments of the project?

A33: Reporting requirements under JFPR are aligned with ADB policies and guidelines.

www.ingramcontent.com/pod-product-compliance
Lightning Source LLC
Chambersburg PA
CBHW050051220326
41599CB00045B/7368